A FALTERING
AMERICAN DREAM

A FALTERING AMERICAN DREAM

Excessive Accumulation of Money and Power
Through the Federal Elections Market

ROBERT W. MERRIAM, PH.D.

ARCHWAY
PUBLISHING

Archway Publishing books may be ordered through booksellers or by contacting:

Archway Publishing
1663 Liberty Drive
Bloomington, IN 47403
www.archwaypublishing.com
1 (888) 242-5904

ISBN: 978-1-4808-2118-7 (sc)
ISBN: 978-1-4808-2117-0 (hc)
ISBN: 978-1-4808-2116-3 (e)

Library of Congress Control Number: 2015950306

Print information available on the last page.

Archway Publishing rev. date: 11/19/2015

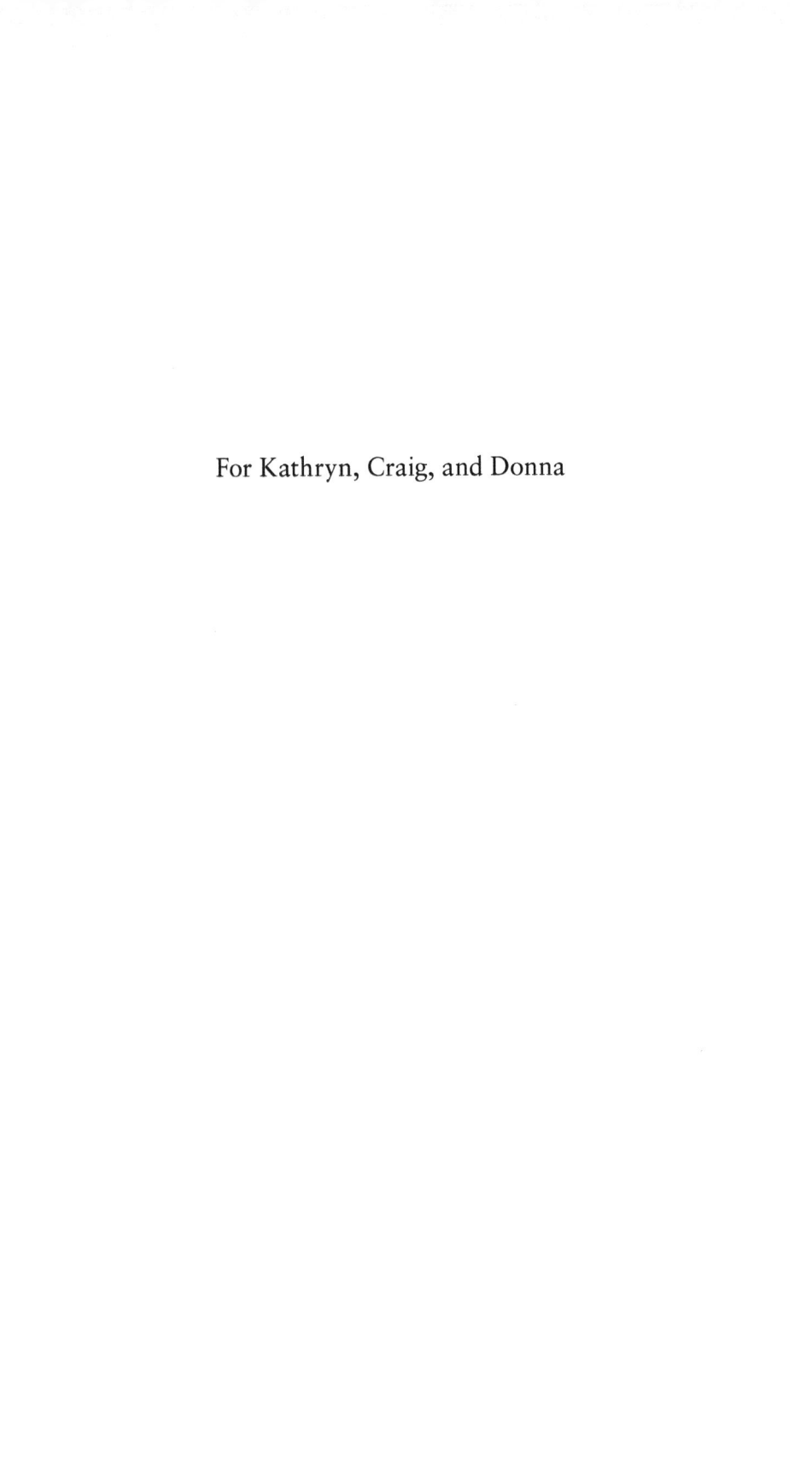

For Kathryn, Craig, and Donna

CONTENTS

GRAPHS

TABLES

ACKNOWLEDGEMENTS

If anything close to wisdom has managed to lodge between my ears, much has been contributed by a continuing conversation over many years with a group of friends. Brought together by membership in a church, representing a wide background of professional experience, and kept together by mutual friendship and respect, their wisdom and insights have truly enriched me. Blaine, Lee, David, Dick (deceased), Bill, and Gary thanks for your many insights and generous friendship.

Ernest Kraybill, Gayle Ruedi, and Ryan Merriam read the book and offered valuable suggestions. Charles Lehman, Monroe Wechsler, and Judith Ferster gave much time and serious help in removing errors and improving the writing and organization. To all of these friends I am seriously in debt while admitting my own responsibility for any factual errors.

"I'm a great believer in the people. If given the truth, they can be depended upon to meet any national crisis. The great point is to bring them the real facts." **Abraham Lincoln**

INTRODUCTION

The arguments advanced in this book are influenced by my long-held convictions. I still believe our form of democracy and its free market economy provide the best way forward but currently need a major adjustment: we need to curb the growing political power of a wealthy oligarchy and restore more governmental sensitivity to the needs of the American people as a whole. I consider the federal government the *only* institution with the power and mandate to achieve and implement fundamental change in the nation.

The foundation of our economy is our middle class with productive jobs for managers and workers in both public and private enterprise. Leaders and workers who work in this economy also happen to constitute the consumers needed in support of it.

Throughout modern history, particularly in the recent past, the failure of an economy has caused personal hardship and a threat to its government. The failure of a national government, however, is much worse: street violence, social chaos, civil war, and regional instability. While maintaining the protections of personal freedoms enshrined in our constitution, the federal government is the only institution capable of achieving all of the national goals specified in that constitution. In an over-populated world, churning with change, our government is not "the problem". It is the only key to national security, economic well-being, and the social stability enabled by a reasonably satisfied citizenry.

The U.S. economy is the central concern around which the issues discussed here revolve. As research for this book progressed, several major themes emerged as central to, and involved in, almost every aspect of our political and economic life. I mention them here to help make connections as you progress through this little book.

One theme arises from what I think should be recognized as the *Great Turning Point*, the point that marked the time when the national debt, as a percent of GDP, ceased going down during thirty-six post-WWII years and started the inexorable increase we still experience today.

Congress recognizes the need for unbudgeted contingencies such as foreign conflicts, terrorism, and natural catastrophes but does not adjust taxes upward to support their costs. World War II was the last time war was officially declared and taxes specifically adjusted upwards on both citizens and businesses to help meet its costs. A lack of political will to raise taxes in support of national responsibilities is a systemic weakness in our form of elected government. Nobody wants taxes, only the security and benefits they bring.

A second theme documents how federal revenues became insufficient after that Great Turning Point and is central to any understanding of how debt increase happens. Therefore, we glance at two contending economic theories that have been tried for stimulating the economy and thus increasing tax revenues. One of those theories consistently has been associated with insufficient tax revenues and mounting debt.

Another theme is a challenge to the widely held notion that costs of governance increase primarily through the effects of inflation and population increase. Actually, costs of governance did parallel these factors fairly well for much of our post-WWII history. It is no longer true. This fact is carefully documented here because of its importance to a national understanding of what new taxation policies must take into account.

Unequal distribution of income and wealth in the U.S. has long been known and recently brought to wider attention by Thomas Piketty in his important book "*Capital in the Twenty-first Century.*" Because of the impact on the nation of this unequal distribution of wealth, I describe in some detail its magnitude and how it happens. I interpret this accumulation of wealth in top U.S. households as a diversion of U.S. financial assets out of the consumption and business investments of goods and services sectors of the economy into financial sector speculations where there are relatively few jobs and small value added in employment and economic production.

A theme that is seldom mentioned in economic discussions is emphasized in this book. It is recognition that the most fundamental requirement for a stable society is a government capable of providing a distribution of national assets that does not allow a class of unemployed, poorly paid and poverty-stricken citizens to become a dissatisfied, homeless or shanty-town part of the national scene. I call a stable citizenry, one not motivated to violent change, a *reasonably satisfied citizenry.*

If a reasonably satisfied citizenry is *not* maintained, world history tells us it is dangerous to a nation's integrity and government. This danger, manifest in many nations today, has been exacerbated by overpopulation and the organization of popular anger enabled by mass communications. This communication capability enables a much lower threshold for organized violence against governments and a higher premium on the necessity for governments to maintain a reasonably satisfied citizenry.

The last theme, without question is the most fundamental and important. It is *the corruption of American governance by the influence of profit-oriented interests with their highly specialized goal of money accumulation.* The current use of money in American political elections enables and protects the wide inequality of ownership of America's financial assets and other wealth. This inequality is detrimental to the American dream where everyone has a chance to 'make it'.

Nothing new in this theme, but I spend much effort describing the unprecedented amounts of money involved in American politics and offering a clearer picture of who supplies it and the places and ways in which it is used. I end up focusing on it, emphasizing the issue's importance to our American egalitarian value system. Because of the increasingly unequal distribution of money in the U.S., you will get arguments here that some redistribution of financial assets must be undertaken, not to punish talented successful people or to lower their life styles, but to reintroduce *far too much* of their working capital back into the jobs of basic research, infrastructure development, education, and the consumer spending that are absolutely essential for an adaptive, growing nation and its economy.

Because I will be talking about amounts, distribution, and uses of 'capital', let me define what I mean by the word. The term 'capital' formally refers to money or products of the economy that can be used to make money, have value and can be used as, or exchanged, for money.

Wealth consists of capital made up both of financial assets (money and readily saleable securities) and tangible assets such as buildings, machinery, software, cars etc.

Financial assets are what I will be talking about in this book: that part of wealth that is available for buying goods or services, selling them, or investing in economic entrepreneurship. These financial assets constitute the circulating blood of the economic body. I shall refer to them as money, working capital, or financial assets.

Political bias of the author must be considered in evaluating a work such as this. My own political biases are as strong as anyone's and need to be exposed up front.

My particular view of what our government should provide is colored by my upbringing in the nineteen thirties and forties. My father, working as an insurance salesman, was hard hit by the Great Depression of the thirties. Echoes of family discipline, enforced when little money was available, are still evident in my adult values and behavior: close the doors to conserve heat; no dessert if you leave food on your plate; don't use too much toilet paper; turn off lights when not in use; mend clothes rather than throw them away; don't hire anything you can do yourself.

Raised in a small town in Iowa, I still retain a strong sense of independence and prefer to accomplish what I am able rather than pay someone else to do it. Independence and conservation of personal, political, and environmental resources remain strong elements of my personal value system.

The pride I have in my country resides importantly in the varied nature of the land. The vast hardwood and conifer forests, prairies, mountains, sea shores, and deserts have always fascinated and drawn me. As a city dweller, I periodically retreat into the natural world as a place to get away from the tensions and demands of professional responsibilities and more hectic city life. As a consequence of these experiences, I consistently value and support our national parks and the general goals of environmental conservation.

Also important to me were the opportunities for a good, low cost public education which made possible my graduation with a Ph.D. degree and job in academic science. My higher education was mostly paid for by a government grateful for my service as an infantry soldier in Europe during the Second World War. My residential expenses at public universities were earned by monitoring undergraduate dormitories and teaching undergraduate laboratories.

As a young professor and researcher with little money, much of the recreation enjoyed by my growing family was provided through public amenities. We hiked the trails of national and state parks and forests, sometimes learning about the surrounding natural wonders and history from ranger naturalists. We canoed rivers and lakes from put-in places provided by public ownership or swam from ocean beaches made available by local municipalities. Because of access to these publically-owned places, my family and I developed an appreciation and love of nature and were able to pass it on to our children.

But my greatest national pride comes from the cornucopia of discoveries made by U.S. scientists and brought to the market places of the world by our world-class engineers, producers, and business entrepreneurs. The heavy representation of Nobel prizes won by United States scientists, economists, and artists is not accidental. It was, and is, made possible by public investments in education and the public infrastructure that supports all.

And just as important has been the continuing government support of basic research through the National Science Foundation, Institutes of Health, national laboratories and space centers. Such research has been foundational in the commercial innovation that underlies the many successes of American business.

I know with certainty that Americans in general and politicians from both ends of the political spectrum all want the same thing: a prosperous, educated, and stable citizenry, supported by a vigorous economy with sufficient jobs to support working-age Americans. We all would like, once again, to see our country regarded at home and abroad as a great nation. In this book I present arguments that our federal government needs to reestablish political sensitivity to *all* Americans with increased resources, not less, to accomplish any goal of national greatness.

PUBLIC SUBSIDIES FOR CORPORATE OPERATIONS

1

Private companies have learned that the need of states for tax revenue from private enterprise is so great that those states are willing to pay companies to operate in their jurisdictions. This has created a competitive market for state tax revenues that ends up redistributing considerable money from state taxpayers to private companies.

L ike the federal government since the middle 1970's, states need more tax revenue. But taxes are claims on our hard-earned money, the stuff of consumption and the foundation of our comfort and security. As naturally as we engage in a quest for the next meal, we exert our best efforts to minimize the removal of this tax money from our private control.

Some are better equipped to succeed in reducing their tax burdens than are others. If some taxpayers succeed in highly effective ways, the rest of us with few tax-avoidance skills will have to pay more to keep our governments going. But, knowing that government services are increasingly important in a job-poor world, we must come to grips with better ways to find tax revenues and distribute their benefits more evenly throughout the nation. So let's start with a look at some legal and highly successful tax-reduction efforts.

Companies used to locate their offices or production facilities in locales where labor was plentiful, state taxes low, and with good proximity of markets and raw materials. They also looked for communities with good schools and other amenities for resident managers and workers.

But today, companies have found that jobs are so scarce and the taxes derived from their operations needed so much that states will compete to give them state tax revenues for locating operations in their jurisdictions. This need has created a competitive market for state tax money or other kinds of donations. Private companies have been quick to exploit this.

The logic is simple: companies will bring jobs, business activity, and tax revenues to a state if it provides competitive incentives. Such an investment by a state may or may not pay off over the long haul. There is no guarantee that the company, subject to unforeseen factors, will flourish or stay.

In the short term, an offer represents an investment of public money to secure business, jobs, and tax revenue over the longer term. A state's investment decision transfers scarce tax revenue to a company's bottom line. Such tax revenue normally is used for public services like education, infrastructure, and social services. The decision to offer such incentives is hard: a short-term speculation on securing a long-term outcome.

Since the Great Recession of 2008, with its reduction in jobs, too many states have had insufficient revenue to maintain their services at optimal levels. In North Carolina, for example, newspaper reporters for Raleigh's *News and Observer* found that cash or tax breaks, as inducements for companies to settle in North Carolina, cost the state about $1 billion a year in tax revenues. This public expenditure is significant, because one must view it in relation to the state legislature's decisions to cut funding for education, health services, social services, and environmental conservation.

Another *News and Observer* report focused on a tax break

for U.S. Airways, assuring it would maintain a hub in Charlotte. The break reportedly saves the airline $8.5 million a year in reduced state tax payments.

Another news story published the contents of a letter that a senior vice president of The Motion Picture Association of America wrote to North Carolina's legislative leaders and governor to promote the continuation of a state incentive program. This program has provided film and TV producers millions in cash payments for working in the state. The letter from the association warned that discontinuing the subsidies would cost North Carolina "tens of thousands of jobs and hundreds of millions of dollars in private business investment" ... and that alleged legislative reluctance to continue the subsidy was ... "already having a negative effect on the state" ... which might mean that North Carolina would ... "no longer be considered for future feature film productions."

This probably was not an idle threat. As of 2011, fifteen states were offering competitive tax credits to filming companies. For the companies, this is just good business. Why spend money on sets and locations at home base when you can reduce production costs by utilizing more natural or less expensive scene locations in well-paying locations? This is a good business argument made possible by the absence of federal laws preventing the flow of public money to private enterprise.

Reporting on the same theme on December 2, 2012, The New York Times emphasized the magnitude and frequency of this competition among states. The journalist, Louise Story, summarized the current market for locating businesses with billions of taxpayer dollars being offered to companies across the country. Her examples include several situations: incentives for auto manufacturing locations had grown to $13.9 billion since 1985; incentives offered by New York State to movie filming companies was found to equal the salaries of 5,000 urgently needed public school teachers; the American International Group (AIG) received $23 million from New York City while being bailed out with $180 billion of federal taxpayer dollars.

Another *New York Times* article (January 26, 2014) provided further indication of the extent of these state inducements: Tennessee provided about $577 million for a Volkswagen manufacturing plant that amounted to $288,500 public dollars per Volkswagen job; Alabama offered a $158 million package of benefits to Airbus.

This brisk business of soliciting public money for bringing private enterprise to a state has generated a separate market for state tax money. Many of the companies receiving tax credits cannot use them because they pay corporate taxes in another state. This poses no problem; companies can sell their in-state tax credits in this new market for eighty to ninety-five cents on the dollar.

In a report on filming companies in the U.S., the *Stamford Advocate* estimated these "tax credit" sales at about $500 million a year. Brokers, coming into this market, buy tax credits from recipient companies, package them, and sell the packaged credits to investors. Brokerage fees in this market are reputed to be substantial.

Awarding tax money to attract more private enterprise to a state has a reasonable basis. After all, the incoming business brings in jobs and potential profits, both of which can be taxed to recoup the tax investment over the long term. States often link their tax credits to actual jobs or income created by the incoming company.

Unfortunately, cost/benefit analyses of these deals show mixed results. Too often the company does not hire many local people or has trouble that prevents anticipated expansion or even long-term viability. A *Stamford Advocate* news reporter concluded in his investigation: "The clear winners are the middle men: tax credit brokers and investors. State governments often just take a leap of faith" about longer-term results.

Although widely used by attracting business, tax-incentive deals also contain a potential for companies to demand more state benefits by threatening to move to another state. Why couldn't a television company with facilities in Iowa, hiring many workers and producing many taxable jobs, tell the state that it needs tax relief or it will have to go elsewhere? In this scenario, the company pleads for help because of fierce competition with slim margins of profit. Since much money is involved, governing authorities will have to listen. If the threat seems plausible, they might accommodate the business even if the practice also seems like out-and-out blackmail.

A recent case in point arose in Washington, home to the Boeing the aircraft company. According to a January 27, 2014, article in the *New York Times*, the company extracted an $8.7 million subsidy from the state in order to keep Boeing in Washington after it threatened to move to a nonunion state.

But companies do operate in a competitive marketplace where decisions about location of facilities in the long run should be dictated by optimizing operations and sales. Also important in a location decision is the quality of the schools and community amenities needed by the company's employees and their families. The sensible solution to this problem of using taxpayers' money as bribes would be a federal law forbidding the practice. As we all know, powerful money-oriented business interests would oppose it in Congress, substantially reducing any hope for getting it through the currently gridlocked chambers.

The needed law, however, could be made business-friendly and more acceptable to members of Congress and their business supporters. It would need a public-friendly section stipulating that states could still compete for a company's location with tax incentives *if* the incentive money rewarded taxpayers' needs as well as the business's needs.

To accomplish this modification of law, state tax incentives could still be offered to a company but only for community improvements specified in a negotiated incentive contract. The state's money designated for the business in the negotiated package would go toward creating or improving community amenities.

This could mean, for example, such things as better-funded school facilities, more support for teachers, and supplies for students. Such support also could create local jobs through public infrastructure improvements and help for supportive local businesses. Perhaps state tax money could be used for permanent company structures that would tie company operations more closely to the local community. Such incentives would directly benefit both company and community and help to justify the transfer of public money to private enterprise. So how might this work?

As happens now, the amount of incentive money would be determined by the size of the company's proposed investment and number and quality of jobs envisioned. State money from this negotiation would be made immediately available to the town or jurisdiction responsible for the negotiated improvements.

Actual work would be awarded by contracts to private companies, while remaining under the control of town authorities, who, by law, would be responsible for seeing that the negotiated work conformed to state and community standards. The company would have controlling oversight to ensure contractual promises were kept. The company also would have the right to claim sponsorship of the improvements and so burnish its brand with the public.

Such a system could be adjusted to make smaller communities more attractive to incoming companies and so help spread commercial activity more broadly over a state rather than allowing further concentration in big cities.

THE INCREASING SUCCESS OF CORPORATE AMERICA IN AVOIDING TAXES

2

Taxes underwrite the government's ability to serve the needs of its citizens. U.S. corporations have used manipulation of national, local, and international tax laws, along with extensive lobbying, to reduce their tax responsibilities. Here, we explore how corporations accomplish this, the magnitude of their efforts, and its harm to government capability.

An executive of Apple Corporation made a statement quoted in the New York Times (1/22/1012) that expressed a basic truth about the goals and interests of big businesses. "We don't have an obligation to solve America's problems. We sell iPhones in over a hundred countries. Our only obligation is making the best product possible." He could have added that the goal of Apple, as in any business, is to maximize profits for owners and investors.

It was a statement of fact that could have come from any business executive: in business there is a necessity to maximize quantity and quality while minimizing production costs. His statement was also an affirmation of American industry that is among the world's best in innovation, production, and the marketing of goods and services here and abroad.

As of this writing, U.S. corporations have a great deal of

cash on hand. According to Birinyi Associates, in 2011 the 500 companies comprising the Standard and Poor index had about $800 billion in cash or equivalents — the most ever at that point. Moody's rating firm that monitors 1,600 companies, reported that their companies had $1.2 trillion in cash at the end of 2010. (To give perspective, one trillion is a million millions.) That aggregate profit had grown eleven percent in one year. Included in these numbers, familiar companies can be identified using 2012 numbers: Apple Corporation had $137 billion in cash equivalents, Microsoft had $78 billion and Cisco $47 billion.

In the operations of the U.S. economy and its businesses, money is the life blood: consumer money for buying goods and services and investment money for business enterprise. In looking at America's money supply, the first thing that jumps out is a vast inequality. In June of 2013 the federal government was in debt to the tune of $16.7 trillion and on track to continue spending more than it receives in tax revenue. The Federal Reserve reported $15.1 trillion in profits held by U.S. corporations in 2011 and this was increasing robustly. An imbalance here is striking. *American corporations are reporting almost as much cash on hand on the profit side of their ledgers as the nation reports on the debit side of its ledger.*

The top tax that U.S. companies face is 35 percent. This is too high by international standards and we often hear it lamented as such in public statements by corporate officials. What corporations actually pay, however, is quite different. It is called their effective tax rate: the percent of profits that actually goes to the tax collector. The money and power of big businesses, working through legal mechanisms and accumulating more and more loophole tax exceptions over time, have greatly reduced the amount of tax money they actually pay.

The *Tax Policy Center* reports that taxes corporations pay have been declining as a percent of GDP for the last twenty years. For example, in 2011 although the legislated rate was 35 percent,

U.S. corporations in the aggregate paid 12.11 percent. That was between 4 and 5 percent less than in the previous year. This tells us that corporate investments in lobbying to reduce their taxes are efficient and on-going.

In comparison with 27 other developed nations, more than half of them had higher *effective* corporate tax rates than the U.S. Thus, in taxes actually paid, U.S. corporations pay less than most other advanced nations. American corporations are not at a tax rate disadvantage with most competitive countries.

Managers of big businesses, like most of us, have a strong motivation to minimize taxes. Their motivation is given power by their resources to hire skillful tax lawyers. This active investment has led to remarkable results. A Government Accounting Office (GAO) report found that 55 percent of big U.S. companies did not pay *any* taxes for at least one year between 1998 and 2005. While corporate profits rebounded far above what they were before the Great Recession of 2008-09, taxes actually paid by corporations are at a historic low. In response to publication of a GAO report on effective taxes paid, Senator Carl Levin remarked, "Today's GAO report quantifies just how much of the corporate tax burden has been shifted onto other taxpayers. America's large profitable corporations are now paying a lower rate than our teachers and firefighters."

The amount of foreign investment by American corporations is considerable. Bloomberg News in a 2012 report, noted that a sample of 70 American companies, out of the thousands with overseas operations, held over a trillion dollars of untaxed profits abroad in various tax havens. In a January 2013 article by Kevin Drawbough of Reuters, the estimated untaxed capital parked overseas by foreign subsidiaries of U.S. corporations was $1.5 trillion. At a 12 percent effective tax rate, that represents $180 billion of lost revenue that year.

In another report by Harry Grubert of the U.S. Treasury Department, the amount of profits earned overseas by 754 big

U.S. multinational corporations was recorded. In the aggregate in 1996, they made 37.1% of their pre-tax profits through foreign subsidiaries. By 2004 their foreign operations were generating 51.1% of all pre-tax profits.

This increase was almost completely in the form of income *not* repatriated and subject to U.S. taxes. Since 2004, more and more corporate operations and profits are being generated abroad while in the U.S. manufacturing, wages, and job creation are less vigorous. This is a significant reason that the stock market is soaring and corporate profits at record highs while U.S. employment levels and wages are recovering much more slowly.

A corporate lobbying effort in the early 2000's was directed at Congress to legislate a tax holiday so that corporate profits, earned and sequestered in tax shelters abroad, could be returned to the U.S. under a lowered U.S. tax requirement. The idea was that returning billions of dollars of foreign profits would result in at least some tax revenue for the government while encouraging corporations to repatriate profits to help their U.S. businesses at home.

The *American Job Creation Act of 2004* resulted. It allowed eligible companies to bring back profits for one year at a 5.25 percent tax rate. The law required that returned capital be used only for domestic investment in the company, not for paying dividends to stockholders or executive compensations. Of the approximate 9,700 companies with foreign subsidiaries, 840 took advantage of the law. What happened?

The companies returned $362 billion of which $312 billion qualified for the tax break. This break gave the companies $254 billion in tax reductions during 2004-06. For this windfall profit, subsequent studies showed little additional money going back into U.S. job creation or business investment. There was, however, an increase in companies buying back shareholder stock.

A follow-up academic study in 2009 found that a large sample of firms taking advantage of the *American Jobs Creation*

Act reaped a 22,000 percent benefit in return for their lobbying investments. These studies make very clear that lobbying the U.S. Congress is a profitable business and demonstrates another role that lobbing money plays in the operation of U.S. tax laws.

Profits from U.S. foreign subsidiaries, parked in foreign tax havens drawing interest, have been earned by American business executives. The ability of most of the managers of these international corporations to produce such foreign profits is the result of education, training, experience, and business connections, developed over time in the United States. Importantly, their foreign operations are protected by the international power of their government. Under the current impasse over tax policy in Congress, few of these foreign profits are available for the taxes that support their government.

In 2008, a report by the *Senate Permanent Subcommittee on Investigations* estimated that the country was losing at least $100 billion a year in corporate tax revenues from foreign operations. The current corporate avoidance of taxes on foreign profits sharply confounds their government's need for revenue and jobs. Unfortunately for the nation, the utilization of low tax foreign jurisdictions for the purpose of tax evasion is increasing rapidly. Tax policy thus needs to be changed to bring tax on foreign-generated profits to some reasonable level and provide a means of actually collecting what is due the government under fair and competitive tax rates.

But offshore tax shelters are not the only means of reducing corporate tax responsibilities. Taxes on big business income vary in the U.S. from state to state, so it is in a company's interest to incorporate in a state with the lowest income tax. Delaware is the most popular state in that regard.

In 2011 Delaware had over 945,000 registered corporations, more than the number of Delaware citizens. These Delaware-registered corporations include such giants as American Airlines, Apple, Bank of America, and Coca Cola. There is a building at 1209 North Orange Street, Wilmington that contains mail drops for all of the 'Delaware' corporations. The state has less restrictive requirements on income disclosure than the Cayman Islands, a popular off-shore tax haven where commercial firms and wealthy individuals hold billions of dollars made in the U.S. economy.

Delaware allows businesses in other states to shift royalties and similar revenues to holding companies in Delaware, where they are not taxed. Over the last ten years, this Delaware loophole allowed corporations to reduce taxes owed to other states by about $9.5 billion. For example, a non-profit *Budget and Policy Center* in Harrisburg, Pennsylvania published a 2004 estimate that this Delaware loophole had cost Pennsylvania $400 million in tax revenue. Two-thirds of the gas extraction companies based in Pittsburg and operating in Pennsylvania happen to be registered at 1209 North Orange St., Wilmington, Delaware.

Senator Carl Levin, over the years, has proposed legislation to force privately owned U.S. corporations to report who actually owns and benefits from their profits. Such legislation could make tax on those profits go to the state of the owner, not Delaware or other tax havens. Every time this legislation has been introduced it has been set aside with the usual criticisms: too costly and burdensome on business while discouraging business investment and thus reducing jobs. Opponents of the bill are giving a higher priority to profit generation than the financial solvency of the United States.

Associated Press correspondents, in an analysis article in 2013, asked an important question: how do corporations score so much profit when the 2013 economy is growing at a slow rate with unemployment at 7.2 percent? This question, at the time, was highly relevant since corporate profits of the second quarter of 2013 were near a record high. The correspondents' answer was that these higher corporate profits were due to cuts in labor, little or no increase in pay for working employees, and additional income from interest on profits held in the U.S. The aggregate pay of American labor in 2013 was near the record low of 2011. So we see that stock markets are soaring, corporate profits at record levels, and profits held abroad are generating income free of U.S. taxation.

Under these circumstances, and with corporate priorities tied to maximizing profit *on investment*, why would corporate executives return foreign profits to the U.S. for taxation? CEO's of large international companies, under this number one rule of business and without government law to retain a reasonable tax, will continue to keep their foreign profits abroad and broaden investments in developing countries where labor costs are low, markets expanding, and profits good.

The large holdings of corporate cash here and abroad are reflected in compensations paid to their executives. The Wall Street Journal published the 2009-2010 compensations (salary plus bonuses of money and/or stock options) of the CEO's of 456 U.S. corporations whose revenue was four billion dollars or more. The total compensation of these managers was $3.9 billion. The average compensation was $8.6 million a year. To put this average in laborers' terms, assuming a 45 hour week and two week vacation, the average compensation comes out to $34,483 a day or $3,831 an hour for an average CEO.

There is an anomaly in current tax law that benefits corporations and their CEO's: companies can subtract the CEO's compensation from their taxable income. Interestingly, there is a provision in the Affordable Care Act that is designed to arrest this tax evasion, at least for executives of health care insurance companies. Executives of those companies cannot deduct more than $500,000 of their compensations from the corporation's taxable income. According to the Congressional *Joint Committee on Taxation*, if this law were to include executive compensations of all U.S. corporations, it would generate around $500 million more in tax revenue each year.

Corporate executives and their advocates argue that these extraordinary executive compensations are justified by the high demands of the job and too few executives with the necessary skills. In service fields of comparable or greater professional demands, U.S. compensations are far lower: the president of the United States earned a basic salary of $400,000 plus perks of the office in 2011 while the speaker of the House of Representative and chief justice of the Supreme Court earned $223,500 each. The median income of presidents of large public universities was $427,000. The Chairman of the Federal Reserve earned $199,700 while presidents of Federal Reserve banks can earn up to $410,780. Top neurosurgeons earned between $250,000 and one million a year. But the difference between compensations of corporate executives and the top earners in all other service fields is in the order of several millions of dollars more per year.

The successful avoidance of corporate tax responsibilities was analyzed by reporters for the New York Times in April, 2012 in the case of Apple Corporation. Apple's tax reduction strategies turned out to involve legal maneuvers common among U.S. multinational corporations. By placing facilities in low-tax jurisdictions, exploiting details of trade agreements among nations, and painstaking interpretation of law, Apple reduced its full U.S. tax of 35% to a mere 9.8% in 2011. This highly compensated legal process of avoiding taxes certainly demonstrates skillful use of the law by tax specialists. It also demonstrates why so many laws and regulations are so lengthy, cumbersome, and time-consuming: a great part of their substance is devoted to trying to eliminate the many clever ways of legally getting around their intent.

Several academic studies have shed light on the extent and effectiveness of corporate lobbying in the U.S. Congress. M.D. Hill and colleagues at the University of Mississippi in 2008 studied the lobbying efforts of a group of S&P firms between 1998 and 2006. They found that the lobbying expenses of the group increased from $1.45 billion to $2.6 billion during those eight years. In the same period their number of registered lobbyists increased from 10,693 to 15,247. Associated with these lobbying investments, however, they found that a lobbying expenditure of $1 was correlated with an increase of shareholder value of $199.

B. K. Richter and colleagues at the University of Texas at Austin in 2008 looked at relationships between the average amount of money a group of corporations spent on tax lobbying and their average reduction in taxes. They found that associated with increases in lobbying was an 18.6 percent reduction in federal tax responsibilities for that group.

But corporate profits rebounding after the Great Recession of 2008-09 have not been accompanied by gains in the U.S. work force. In the aggregate, U.S. labor wages were at least 50% of GDP until 1975 but since then this percentage has been falling. In the second quarter of 2013 workers' wages were a historic low at 43.5 % of GDP. Since the recession of 2008, economic growth and corporate profit have far outpaced the U.S. aggregate hourly wage.

So how is the corporate world doing? As of the third quarter of 2012 their aggregate earnings were $1.75 trillion. Although this number speaks well of their current efforts in domestic and world markets, we may be sure their lobbyists are busy, asking Congress for tax and regulatory relief in brutally fierce and competitive world markets.

BASIC IDEAS THAT INFLUENCE ECONOMIC POLICIES FOR DEMOCRATS AND REPUBLICANS

3

The two political parties differ strongly on methods of stimulating the economy to relieve business recessions. These differences stem from ideas of two prominent economists of the last century. Here is a quick outline of the principal ideas underlying current political debate and rancor.

Public pronouncements by Republicans place the blame for the high national debt on tax and spend policies of Democrats. In the current job-poor recovery from the 2008 recession, Republicans want to reduce federal expenditures especially on social programs, resisting further borrowing and increase of the national debt. Political right-leaning advocates often character-ize jobless people as takers who would rather take government subsidies than find a job and support themselves. They point out that such hand-out programs encourage dependency, not self-sufficiency.

To stimulate a lagging economy, Republicans want to reduce income taxes to give those with jobs more money to spend, know-ing that it is consumer spending that supports and stimulates the economy. Republicans also claim that excessive government regulations impede business activity and must be reduced. They regard government as the institution that takes away their profits in taxes and clutters the road to profit with regulations.

Democrats point out that it was *under*-regulation of high-profit, high-risk financial speculation that precipitated the financial collapse of 1929, the Great Depression of the 1930's, and the recent Great Recession of 2008. To regenerate a recessed economy, they prefer federal programs that borrow money to prevent the collapse of financial institutions and support the economy by supplying jobs or the means of buying necessities for people out of work. They argue that such relief eases poverty for people who will spend every dollar supplied to them for necessities in the goods and services economy. They affirm that increased consumer spending is what stimulates the economy, allowing business investment. They look to a regenerating economy to provide the economic growth that allows a slow repayment of the national investment in consumer spending.

The means of stimulating a recessed economy is thus seriously contended by the parties, each advocating economic theories that go back to the early 20th century. The left favors ideas promulgated by John Maynard Keynes, a leading Scottish economist of the time.

Keynesian theory looks to government spending as the best tool for bolstering the consumer base of a struggling economy: public borrowing to fund jobs or economic relief for the unemployed. In the recent recession it entailed such things as food stamps and unemployment insurance. Under President Franklin Roosevelt in the 1930's, it involved public funding of jobs that built public amenities such as roads, water and irrigation systems and maintained the educational base as well as basic research and trade skills. Democrats maintain that this economic boost, if done adequately, will relieve the human pains of poverty, stimulate the economy, maintain infrastructure and work skills, and eventually revitalize the economy.

The Republican view of economic stimulation is traceable to the Austrian economist, Friedrich Hayek, also of the early 20th century. Hayek was particularly concerned about the inflation that can result from government borrowing or printing of money. He had experienced destructive inflation in Austria and Germany after the First World War when the conquered countries' central banks printed money but had few tools for containing inflation. In 1919 an American dollar bought 16.1 Austrian crowns. By 1923 it bought 70,800 crowns. This disastrous situation generated a fear of inflation in Hayek that strongly inclined him toward sound money, low-debt policies.

Using Hayek's ideas, Republicans object to increasing debt through borrowing during recessions. In recessed times of reduced tax revenues and higher unemployment, Republicans favor reducing debt by reducing government spending: reducing services and putting off infrastructure needs. For economic stimulation they favor reduction of taxes for consumers with jobs, giving them more money to buy and support the goods and services economy. The additional consumer spending should increase tax revenues from increased business activity, offsetting revenue reduction due to lowered tax rates.

As we shall see, the economic ideas of Keynes and Hayek have been tested in U.S. history. President Franklin Roosevelt tried Keynesian theories to legislate government borrowing, enabling him to fund jobs during the Great Depression of the 1930's, during which military production caused by the Second World War forced even greater borrowing and spending.

President Ronald Reagan tried Hayek's ideas by lowering taxes during a serious economic downturn in the early 1980's. It will be interesting to see what actually happened in each experiment.

THE TWO POLITICAL PARTIES TRY DIFFERENT WAYS TO STIMULATE THE ECONOMY DURING RECESSIONARY DOWNTURNS

4

The economic damage and personal misery caused by the market crash of 1929 and the Great Depression of the 1930's was mitigated by employing the unemployed. The government borrowed money to create jobs and stimulate the economy. In the serious business recession of the early 1980's, President Reagan lowered income taxes on employed workers to increase consumption and stimulate the economy. Here, we take a careful look at how these two great economic experiments played out.

In current contentions, both political parties recognize the importance of the consumer base. When consumer confidence and spending fall off for any reason, businesses see decreases in sales and respond by cutting labor costs and production. This in turn increases unemployment and further reduces the consumer base, creating a downward recessionary spiral. Members of both political parties further agree that recovery of the economy is essential but sparks fly when how to stimulate the economy is debated. That is the point where the two parties back off into seemingly non-negotiable positions.

After the market crash of 1929, the resulting Great Depression cut a grim swath through what was left of the American economy. In 1929 the wealth of the nation was heavily concentrated at the very top of the wealth spectrum as it is today. When the big financial institutions crashed in '29, it was rich investors who felt it first. Under President Herbert Hoover, a staunchly conservative Republican, there was no bailout of banks and little stimulus spending provided by the Congress to keep some of the work force employed and consumer spending supported. Wealthy investors, now poor, sometimes found themselves on the street, selling pencils or apples. Freight trains became the vehicle of necessity for unemployed workers going somewhere, anywhere, to find a job. Hobo camps full of unemployed men on the move sprang up at railroad sidings near cities.

President Franklin Roosevelt, inheriting this severely depressed economy in 1933, set about to create jobs and consumers for the economy. To do this he drew on the theories of John Maynard Keynes: borrow money to create jobs and through their wages increase economic consumption to support businesses and stimulate the economy. Money borrowed to do this would be paid back gradually when the economy was again humming with good tax revenues.

By 1933 economic pain was intense and President Roosevelt didn't waste much time after taking office. One of his first creations was cobbled together from existing army equipment, plans and leadership. His Civilian Conservation Corps (CCC) was created and given an army organization plan, leadership, and facilities.

Army discipline prevailed at CCC camps: reveille in the morning before breakfast when the flag was raised, taps before

bed in the evenings when the flag was lowered. At each cere-
mony the men, in civilian clothes, stood in ranks to be counted.
Army food was plentiful and hearty. The men in CCC camps did
public work. They helped manage national forests, built public
parks, trails, roads, and other recreational and municipal facilities across the nation.

The quality of work done was first class, directed by unemployed professional engineers and craftsmen. If you ever encoun-
ter a beautifully built building with superb stone walls in an old
public park, it probably is a structure built by CCC men back
in 1933-39.

Another public works program in those desperate years was
the Work Progress Administration (WPA). This program offered
employment that supported and helped preserve creative occupa-
tions like craftsmanship, writing, drafting, and artistic skills. Some
top Broadway musicals were produced and staged, for example.
Both the CCC and WPA programs offered paid opportunity for
enrollees to develop, enhance, or maintain their skills. The pay for
individuals was small so every dollar of public wage went directly
into purchases in the goods and services economy for maximum
economic stimulus. There was no discretionary money left over
for financial speculation to enhance incomes of the well-employed.

The corollary to these expenditures, of course, was government borrowing and a growing national debt. In the 1930's,
as today, debt-conscious Congressional legislators resisted borrowing and increasing public debt. With stimulus money the
Roosevelt administration was able to get through Congress, the
depression was never fully reversed but much was accomplished.
Public amenities were created or maintained, manual and artistic
skills were maintained or developed, countless families were kept
out of soup kitchens, and many businesses were kept alive. It
was left to the Japanese attack on Pearl Harbor to really awaken
a national consciousness that finally overcame Congressional
reluctance to borrow.

With the aggressions of Germany and Italy in Europe and Japan in Asia, the U.S. government began to borrow from its citizens through sale of war bonds to prepare for the worst. This money was used to rebuild the industrial base that would be needed if war came. In December of 1941 when the Japanese attacked Pearl Harbor, the country swung into a highly managed economy with price-fixing, conscripted mobilization of military and industrial services, and rationing of scarce foods and war materials.

With the declaration of war, Congress *enacted new taxes* to help pay for the increased expenditures. There was little political outcry about creeping socialism as national concern trumped political propaganda. People accepted much higher taxes as a necessary hardship. Despite the sharply increased income taxes, however, the national debt ballooned as war engulfed the world.

By the war's end in 1945, the national debt was a greater percent of the GDP than the debt of 2009. Despite the massive increase in debt, however, a highly productive economy was now roaring like a river in flood. Unlike today, political parties found common purpose in war efforts so that Congress was able to act.

Tax on top incomes increased to 94 percent during the war and never went lower than 70 percent until 1981. A sufficiently-funded federal government provided premier services and was able to make foreign and domestic investments that set the U.S. apart as a world leader. Nothing close to socialism happened and the national debt was at a comfortable percent of GDP when Jimmy Carter ended his presidency in 1981.

The economic chaos of those war years has made possible alternate interpretations of almost everything that happened during the war and after. Still, we can say with complete confidence that high government borrowing and spending for war production produced revitalized manufacturing facilities and a highly productive economy with full employment.

The growing economy after the war was helped by the fact

that much potentially competitive European production had been destroyed by the war. And it was this vigorous economy that made reduction of the huge post-war debt possible while still supporting generous government investments in education of its veterans, modernization of public infrastructure, and cutting-edge scientific progress. Those public investments produced scientific momentum second to none and made possible the space program, a superb national park system, interstate highways, a scientific enterprise second to none, and many other sources of national pride. America led and was widely admired through its government's actions at home and abroad.

At this point, we turn to an equally bold economic stimulus plan enacted by President Ronald Reagan's administration in the 1980's that has become the touch stone of Republican economic policies ever since. This plan was founded on ideas of sound money and free markets with low inflation articulated convincingly by Friedrich Hayek and others in the University of Chicago economics department.

Reagan took office in a recessed business cycle with lowered GDP and high unemployment. His idea: expand economic growth, not by borrowing and spending on more jobs, but by reducing government services and jobs and cutting taxes which would put more spending money into the pockets of people with incomes.

Additionally, tax cuts on high incomes would provide more money for business investors that would translate into more jobs. The increased consumption caused by lowered income taxes would stimulate the economy and maintain or increase tax revenues. A political bonus, of course, was that lowered taxes would certainly be popular in election politics. It would be a win-win-win strategy for Republicans: boost the economy, minimize national debt and win elections. An important part of this concept was the expectation that increases in consumer spending and business investments would result in more business tax revenue to offset lowered rates of taxation.

Since Reagan's time, an observation by the economist Arthur Laffer has been used to support Reagan's idea: as taxes are raised, wealthy taxpayers increasingly find ways to shelter their income from taxes, reducing the amount of tax revenue. The theoretical corollary is that as taxes are lowered, more income from private sources is made available for taxation. Subsequent Republican administrations, benefiting from the popularity of lower taxes and some consequences of the Laffer effect, have continued this strategy.

More recently, under coercive political threats by the Republican activist Grover Norquist, Republicans, at least within the extreme right wing of the party, have elevated a no-new-taxes mantra to a no-compromise status: no tax increases at all under pain of party banishment and well-funded competition in primary elections by more active tax-avoidance Republican candidates. What were the economic consequences of Reagan's great experiment?

In carrying out his experiment, President Reagan signed into law the "Economic Recovery Tax Act of 1981." Taxes on top incomes were reduced from 70% to 50% and finally to 28% in his eight years. A crucial part of the Reagan idea is the expectation that the economic impetus resulting from tax cuts would stimulate business, increasing taxable profits and income.

Graph 1 shows tax rates on top incomes, along with inflation-adjusted federal expenditures and tax revenues from a few years before Reagan's experiment to its end: 1974 to 1989.

What we see is that tax revenues took a sharp drop in 1981 – 83. The Congressional Budget Office calculated the decrease in revenue at about 13 percent below what would have been expected without the tax cuts. Unfortunately for the nation, however, although revenues fell, federal expenditures were increased by the Reagan administration, particularly military expenditures justified by the cold war with Russia. President Reagan left his presidency with the national debt, as a percent of GDP, much greater than when he took over. This "great turning point" was a highly significant change from the decreases that had been continuously achieved by both party administrations since 1945.

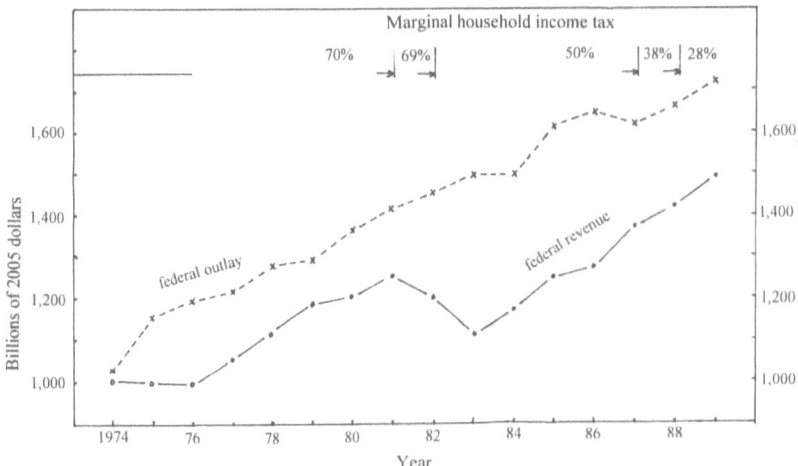

Graph 1   Federal expenditures and revenues in billions of inflation-adjusted dollars 1974-89. Data from the Tax Policy Center, "Historical Federal Receipt and Outlay Summary."

The graph demonstrates a difference between revenues and expenditures that widened significantly between 1981 and 1983. This increased deficit spending has continued through the years up to the present, reversed for only four years of deficit reduction under President Clinton. In his administration, taxes on top incomes were increased, expenditure increases slowed, and the effects of an economic technology boom helped with revenues.

The economic stimulation expected by President Reagan did occur. New and unfilled orders for U.S. industries rose 36 percent from the previous Carter years. Before-tax profits of corporations increased 31 percent and the average growth rate of GDP was almost as good as that of the two previous, non-recession administrations. By these measures President Reagan was right:

economic stimulation indeed did occur when he cut income taxes on those who were still employed.

These advances in business activity did not translate into worker benefits however. Unemployment under the previous Ford and Carter administrations averaged 6.6% but increased to 7.5% during Reagan's time. Those stuck at or below the poverty level averaged 11.7% of workers during the Ford and Carter terms but increased to 14.0% during Reagan's watch. And despite increased business activity, the average hourly earnings of workers increased only 28%, much below the 80% increase during the previous Ford and Carter years.

In these measurements of economic health we see business profits increasing without similar increases in workers' wages. This is painfully similar to statistics in the recent 2009 – 2014 period: business profits and GDP gains increasing robustly while workers' benefits in jobs and wages stagnate or decline. At this point we might ask where the profits went from these increases in business activity and profits during the Reagan terms.

The high rates of taxation of the wealthy during and after WWII had reduced the amount of national wealth owned by the top 1% from a high of 44.2 percent before the market crash of 1929 to 20.5 percent by the end of the Carter Administration in 1980. According to the economist G. Wm. Domhoff, after President Reagan lowered income taxes, the U.S. wealth owned by the top 1 percent, increased from 20.5 to 35.7 percent by the end of his two terms. This informs us that most of the profits generated during this period went to the wealthiest households, especially the top one percent. This was wealth trickling upward.

According to Federal Reserve data, President Reagan's terms also coincided with huge increases in the amount of U.S. capital dedicated to financial speculation. From 1950 to 1980, financial assets in the U.S. amounted to about four times GDP. By 2008 U.S. financial assets had increased to ten times GDP. In a later chapter we shall consider the enormous significance of this growing size of American capital directed to financial sectors and the growing inequality in holders of U.S. wealth.

The most obvious effect of the Reagan low tax initiative, however, was the increase in the national debt due to his increase in expenditures and decrease in tax revenues. At the time Reagan started lowering taxes in 1981 the national debt had been reduced under the administrations of seven administrations from a 1946 level of 117.5% of GDP to 32.5% by 1980. This debt reduction was achieved by both Republican and Democratic administrations with Congresses still capable of compromise and progress.

In summary, how has President Reagan's idea of lowering taxes worked out for the economy? He was not correct that lowered taxes would result in the same or higher tax revenues. There were, however, increases in business profits and GDP. Increased federal spending initiated a dramatic increase in borrowing and size of the national debt. Unfortunately, the profits from increases in GDP and business activity did not 'trickle down' to working consumers but up to top earners. The rate of new job creation and wage increases stagnated or went down while unemployment and levels of poverty went up.

For the top 1% of earners, the Reagan low tax idea increased their share of national wealth. This increase in wealth signified that the extra tax money given to these top earners by President Reagan was not spent in the goods and services sectors where jobs, business activity, and consumption were needed. Rather, most of it was invested in wealth-increasing financial assets. In the years during and since President Reagan's two terms, tax revenues have slipped further and further behind expenditures so that under Republican low tax policies the national debt has continually increased even as GDP has grown.

At this point I want to highlight this dramatic turning point in our funding of the federal government. From the end of WWII until President Reagan's great experiment, national debt was slowly and continually decreased under higher taxation of top incomes. The percent of national wealth accumulated by top-earning households was kept much lower than before the crash of 1929.

With lowered taxation of high incomes under President Reagan and their continuation by the two Bush administrations, debt has continually increased. Because of its importance to understanding taxes and debt, I will emphasize this reversal of sufficient federal funding in the 1980's as the 'Great Turning Point' in our nation's economic history.

Of these two experiments in economic stimulation, the Keynesian approach of President Roosevelt clearly gave the best results for economic stimulation, given that the higher tax revenues from higher incomes in the revitalized economy eventually were adequate to both reduce the public debt *and* allow investment in world class public amenities.

His hiring of the unemployed to accomplish public work seems to me a better way to help the unemployed than the temporary 'free-money' relief being offered today by programs such as food stamps and unemployment insurance. Although 'free-money' programs will always be needed for elderly and disabled Americans, real employment of labor for the maintenance and improvement of public facilities would be a more productive way to support and maintain skills for the able-bodied unemployed.

Public amenities have to be regularly maintained and improved. Why not mitigate business cycle recessions by increased public investments in labor to smooth out a GDP decline and in so doing maintain and upgrade worker skills and motivations? This would be possible with federal revenues more in line with the taxation policies of the 1950 - 1980's.

THE TIGHT RELATIONSHIP BETWEEN BUSINESS AND GOVERNMENT IN THE GLOBAL ECONOMY

5

The national government and American businesses are not antagonistic, but in fact closely cooperating and mutually dependent. Their purposes and responsibilities, however, are hugely different.

G lobalization, brought on by advances in communications, transportation, and emerging overseas markets has encouraged U.S. business investment in international consumer and labor markets. This globalized outreach is providing American companies with important market expansions. Access to cheaper foreign labor, coupled with American manufacturing know-how, has enabled the production and sale of less expensive goods and services in markets here and abroad.

A down side, however, is that utilization of cheaper foreign labor has contributed to the loss of much U.S. manufacturing and the associated jobs. Those jobs provided the better incomes that defined and sustained much of the American middle class in the post-WWII years. Wage stagnation for U.S. workers over the last three decades has been substantially due to this outsourcing of manufacturing jobs to foreign countries. Immigration into the U.S. of laborers from countries with lower-pay expectations and the weakening of labor unions here in America also have put downward pressure on wages for American workers.

The higher cost of U.S. manufacturing labor also has motivated companies here in the U.S. to replace what is left of domestic labor with automation, computer programing, and robotics. Today, advances in robotic and computer-driven machines are surprisingly rapid. With the further development of artificial intelligence and manual dexterity, machines are taking over more and more of the operations of manufacturing, office work, and other jobs traditionally done by humans. This has increased productivity for businesses, increased profits, and lowered prices for their products.

From a national perspective, however, this loss of jobs is the exact opposite to the job creation the nation needs. Thus, globalization has exposed and exacerbated a growing divide between the legitimate goals and needs of U.S. multinational corporations and their government. This divide is not a fault of either business or government. Rather, it reflects the characteristics of a free market that, if projected into the future unaddressed, predicts bad outcomes for both business and government.

Another effect of globalization impacts government revenues and services. It is required of government to run its national services, maintain a reasonably satisfied citizenry, and protect American commercial and tourist interests at home and abroad. As explained earlier, however, U.S. corporations exploit foreign tax havens and international trade agreements to reduce their U.S. taxes. Such efforts have been highly successful even as corporate profits are at historic highs and the national debt is at a level that helps fuel political deadlock in Washington.

Because Democratic administrations are continuously criticized by Republican politicians as antagonistic to business interests through taxation and regulations, it would be well to recall for a moment something we hear too little about: the necessary and intimate relationship that actually exists between governments and their business communities.

Despite mutual dependence, the goals of the two partners are starkly different. For-profit businesses have relatively simple goals: investment of capital to create or supply consumer demand, burnish the company brand, and maximize return on investment. For publically owned companies, their investors also are primarily concerned with return on investment.

The U.S. government, on the other hand, is shaped by, and sensitive to, taxpaying and voting citizens with an enormously wide range of capabilities, needs, and desires. As if this diverse range of needs were not enough, the government also must deal with international environments where competing economies and religions, conflicts of national interests, wars, and natural disasters demand our government's involvement abroad in the interests of American economic well-being and physical security.

Responsible for every aspect of the country in a violent and competitive world, government also supplies what U.S. business could not exist without: hundreds of millions of consuming citizens who still happen to be one of the most reliable customer markets in the world market place. Businesses also depend on the expensive, government-maintained legal marketplace that ensures fair competition and practices between businesses, customers, and competitors.

Government help for businesses comes through lowered taxes in response to specific company needs and through help for start-up businesses by the Small Business Administration and other federal and state agencies. When corporations fail and the economy is collapsing, only the government has the power and resources to rescue mega corporations and the economy.

Introduction of high tech products into markets couldn't happen without the fundamental research that underlies the final development and engineering of high tech products. This basic research, overwhelmingly funded by government, takes place mostly in universities and government programs in space exploration, health science, environmental science, and military technology.

Spin-offs from such programs have been crucial in bringing new products to the world's market places. Contrary to political complaints about government hostility to businesses through taxes and regulations, it is in the government's interest to do all it can to support American businesses, both large and small. It does so in a multitude of ways, providing support of many kinds for every kind of legal enterprise in the country and abroad.

As innovative, efficient, and affluent as business leaders may be, their goals and expertise are relatively narrow in scope. And unfortunately, practices of large businesses, operating in global free markets, are too often in direct conflict with what the nation needs: good-paying manufacturing jobs and return of reasonable tax revenue in support their government and their American consumers.

There is at present an alledged shortage of U.S. workers trained in advanced industrial production, especially in the manufacture and operation of advanced production machinery. A technically trained work force is essential for both corporate high tech enterprise and the nation's need for high quality manufacturing jobs *here in the U.S.* The expansion of this kind of training most probably will be dependent on collaboration between government and businesses.

Many of today's unemployed are experienced middle aged workers who have trouble finding work in which their older skills are valuable. Some are young, educated to varying degrees, and qualified for better jobs than the low level service jobs currently available. So, how can we provide advanced training for higher tech employment that enables manufacturing and utilizes American workers? And how can we do this without creating new, expensive institutions or introducing training courses into colleges and universities that would displace their highly important liberal arts general education?

An apprentice system that honed craft skills generations ago, has been modified today in Germany to provide a higher degree of training for mechanized and computerized fabrication work than is available in educational institutions. Modified apprentice training might also be workable in this country.

In a modified apprentice concept, the federal government might fund training grants in the states through State Apprenticeship Offices (SAO). Such program offices would not displace on-going state or local employment services or training programs at community colleges and technology schools. The SAO offices would act to add new training capability specific to companies' particular technical needs.

Employers, private or public, who need workers with specialized skills would list openings with requirements through the SAO's. A person needing a job or wanting a better one could look over the state SAO list. If that person could find an employer whose requirements seemed attainable, an application with a resume would be sent. If the employer felt the applicant's resume looked promising, an interview would be scheduled. The employer would make a decision and an offer could be made for the SAO program.

In such a program there would be a need for pre-determined guidelines specifying how long an apprenticeship would be funded, depending on the nature of technical skills required. Within these guidelines, the program would pay some portion of the wage the employer would offer for an employee for those skills. The program contribution to the wage might be tapered, beginning with a higher proportion of the stipulated wage at the beginning and tapering off in one or two increments to zero at the conclusion of the training period.

From the beginning of the apprenticeship, it would be

understood by contract that on conclusion of a successful training period, the employer would employ the trainee at the stipulated wage for at least some pre-determined period or, if unsatisfied with accomplishment or potential during training at any time, could send the trainee back into the labor market with a letter explaining the level of technical training attained.

The higher and longer the level of training needed, the greater would be the advantage to both employer and trainee. Over time such a program would act to continuously advance, diversify, and upgrade the skills of the American work force, make possible more advanced manufacturing enterprise in this country, and help expand the overall capability of the U.S. economy and its domestic work force. A program like this would continue and expand a long list of public/private collaborations that have served both country and businesses well for generations.

I think most of us would agree that our nation needs more and better collaboration between public and private sectors rather than feelings of "government is the problem" or that business is just organized greed for ever more money.

COMPARING DEMOCRATIC AND REPUBLICAN ECONOMIC POLICIES BETWEEN 1945 AND 2009

6

When they captured the presidency and its executive departments, which party can point to their economic policies as providing the best economic and work force outcomes for the nation?

We have glanced at basic economic theories that motivate and divide the two parties. I described the ways Democratic and Republican administrations responded to economic downturns and general results of their responses to them. Here, I take a simple statistical view of their records, examining the economic records of the two parties over the sixty-four years from the end of the Second World War in 1945 until 2009. I have not included the economic picture after the Great Recession of 2008 because of the unusual, emergency nature of government expenditures at that point.

The period chosen includes both business downturns and boom times, wars, and congressional majorities supportive and opposed to the administration in power. This study used historical data from one government source, *"Economic Report of the President 2012."* This is an annual report to Congress from the executive branch of government.

Taking the numbers for each year of Democratic or Republican four-year presidential terms, I calculated an overall numerical average over the entire 64 year period for each party. The period included the administrations of twelve presidents. Not all tables of the *Economic Report* covered the entire period of this study. All available data between those dates were included.

It is true that some presidents were more adept than others in working with Congress to get their agendas enacted. And a Congress controlled by an opposing party could repress presidential policies. Still, it is party policies functionally executed during a presidential term that mostly direct what happens during a four year term. The accumulated data do not reach the status of statistical proof because of the many variables involved but do deserve a serious look because they average data even-handedly from so many administrations over so many years.

Republican policies assert that smaller federal government is better federal government. President Reagan's remark that government is the problem famously expresses the idea. This party position, repeated endlessly over the years, predicts that increases in government size and expenditure during Democratic administrations will be greater than those under the more conservative policies of Republican administrations. Here are the statistical results in which the aggregate numbers of Republican and Democrat administrations are compared.

Question: What was the *average* percent change in *number of non-military federal employees* per four-year term during seven Democratic and seven Republican administrations, 1946 – 2001? Answer: Democratic = 0.8% *decrease* per term. Republican = 1.3% *increase* per term.

Question: What was the average percent change per term in the *non-military federal payrolls* during seven Democratic and seven Republican administrations, 1946 – 2001? Answer: Democratic = 15.7% *increase* per term. Republican = 17.2% *increase* per term.

Republicans emphasize the national debt as an immediate problem while Democrats regard it as a more long-term problem. Both parties, during the time they held the presidency from 1945 to the early 80's, helped to lower a national debt, initially a greater percent of GDP than the debt of 2009.

Question: What was the average *dollars per term spent in excess of tax revenues* in the terms of seven Democratic and seven Republican administrations 1946 – 2001? Answer: Democratic = $22.4 billion per term. Republican = $124.7 billion per term.

Question: The national debt, as percent of GDP, was reduced during the period 1945 to 1981 by both Democratic and Republican administrations. What was the average percent *reduction in debt per term* of five Democratic and four Republican administrations? Answer: Democratic = 13.2% reduction per term. Republican = 4.74% reduction per term.

Question: What was the percent *cumulative increase in national debt,* as percent of GDP, during seven Democratic and nine Republican administrations, 1945 – 2009? Answer: Democratic = 0.00% increase. Republican = 62.9% increase.

Adequate funding of government depends on a vigorous economy. Both parties agree that this is the case but differ as to how to achieve that vigor. So it was important to look at factors that reflect economic vigor.

Question: What was the average *percent unemployment* during a four year term (or half term), during 6.5 Democratic and 9 Republican administrations, 1948 -2009?
Answer: Democratic = 4.8% unemployed per term. Republican = 6.2% unemployed per term.

Question: What was the average percent *growth in GDP per year* during terms of 4 Democratic and 5 Republican administrations, 1962 to 2009?
Answer: Democratic = 3.2% GDP growth per year. Republican = 1.8% GDP growth per year.

Question: What was the average percent *increase of corporate before-tax profits* of four year terms relative to the previous four year terms of 4 Democratic and 5 Republican administrations, 1962 - 2009?
Answer: Democrat = 41.8% increase. Republican = 23.3% increase.

I make no claims of proof for inferences or conclusions drawn from these numbers. Any credibility lies in the number of administrations averaged over the years. As a whole, they indicate that Republicans, who celebrate the virtues of small government, decry the evils of large national debt and claim the role of business-friendly, GDP-enhancing government, should be careful about such claims. Their numbers since the Second World War do not support claims of preeminence in these categories.

These data suggest that, over the long haul, Democratic policies are associated with smaller government growth, better employment outcomes, smaller budget deficits, and more profitable businesses than do Republicans during the period studied. Reasons for this apparent disparity remain obscure and should be investigated in detail by economists in this field.

INCREASING COSTS AND COMPLEXITY OF NATIONAL GOVERNANCE

7

The costs of government services and obligations are going up faster than the population, inflation and GDP. This trajectory invites scrutiny: Where do these increasing costs come from? Are they necessary?

B oth Democrats and Republicans like to tell voters that government should be as lean as possible. Democrats seem more aware that the spectrum of citizens includes helpless and less capable individuals at the bottom as well as efficiency-driven producers and strivers at the top. Republicans like to focus on business success as the key to almost every problem and that government taxes and regulations on businesses are should be reduced as much as possible.

Both parties, however, look to government to maintain a vigorous market place that ensures fairness and legality, as well as helping to keep U.S. enterprise safe in world markets. Democrats like to emphasize that government has an obligation to ensure a sufficiently equitable distribution of national wealth to prevent formation of a permanent underclass: shanty towns around major cities, or mobs of under-served or excluded and angry citizens in the streets.

Although it has not always been so, far right Republicans

especially are sounding a strident mantra: Government is the problem. Reduce it. If you raise taxes to support it we'll remove you from office at the next election! The call to minimize government has become, over the last few years, more actively promoted by far right Tea-Party Republicans. This rhetoric expresses conservatism that wants minimal government. For these conservatives, federal government needs to be reduced and replaced by more efficient, profit-driven private enterprise with reduction of regulatory oversight.

This trend has accelerated in states with Republican governors, such as an assault on state workers by Governor Scott Walker in Wisconsin. His Act 10 law makes the financing of the state budget possible, without tax increases, by extracting more money from state workers through increasing their contribution to their health plans and by pay freezes.

This act not only degrades public service but also takes away public employee unions' right to bargain over pension, health coverage, safety, hours of work, sick leave, and vacations. Public employee unions are left with bargaining rights only over wages and even that is restricted to raises no greater than increases in inflation. Removing almost all union power, the law has removed the incentive for workers to join and pay union dues, causing widespread loss of union membership and power. Rather than raise more tax revenue, this law balances state budgets by maintaining or cutting the comparatively low compensations paid to teachers and other public servants.

Republicans like to remind voters that earning money from productive work is one of the strongest of human motivations. They tell us that give-away government programs over time, even if seemingly based on intractable social conditions, incline recipients to lethargy and dependence. This is a contention worth consideration.

Given party contentions over government size and regulation, what can we learn about the nature of the seemingly endless laws and regulations that underlie government responsibilities, funding, oversight, and services?

To gain insight, I used statistical data from federal government departments that show federal expenditures per year from 1974 to 2008. Each year's expenditure was first adjusted to remove the effects of inflation. The inflation-adjusted expenditures were then further calculated as federal expenditures per citizen. If inflation and population increases were the only factors causing the increases of federal expenditures each year, expenditures would be a straight line across a graph showing little or no increase.

Graph 2 shows, however, smooth increases in expenditures *per capita* every year. During the years covered, administration priorities and policies changed, dominance of Congress by the parties changed, wars, business downturns and boom economies came and went but the government cost per person doesn't fluctuate much year to year like most single factor variables. It just keeps increasing, showing little evidence of immediate impact from differing government policies. The *rate* of increase per person does vary somewhat, no doubt reflecting effects of political maneuvering, wars, natural catastrophes, new laws, and unexpected expenses.

What causes this relentless increase of costs per person? For starters, it means that presidents and congresses, when campaign promises are over and they confront operational problems in detail, there is little wiggle room for reduction of services that are fulfilling needs identified over time as government responsibilities. Most of these increasing costs are *budgeted* increases, proposed and justified by presidents and executive departments, questioned and passed by Congresses dominated at various times by either party.

One obvious need for government expenditures is the creation and operation of safety net programs to keep poorer or disadvantaged Americans from abject poverty. In 2009, for example, the country was suffering from massive job loss due to the Great Recession of 2008. Dozens of programs, such as food stamps and Medicare, were expanded, providing an average of $6,583 for every person, a 69 percent increase per person since 2000. These statistics are grim and highlight the fact that there were insufficient job opportunities by 2009 to provide enough families with basic needs such as food, housing, health care, and schooling.

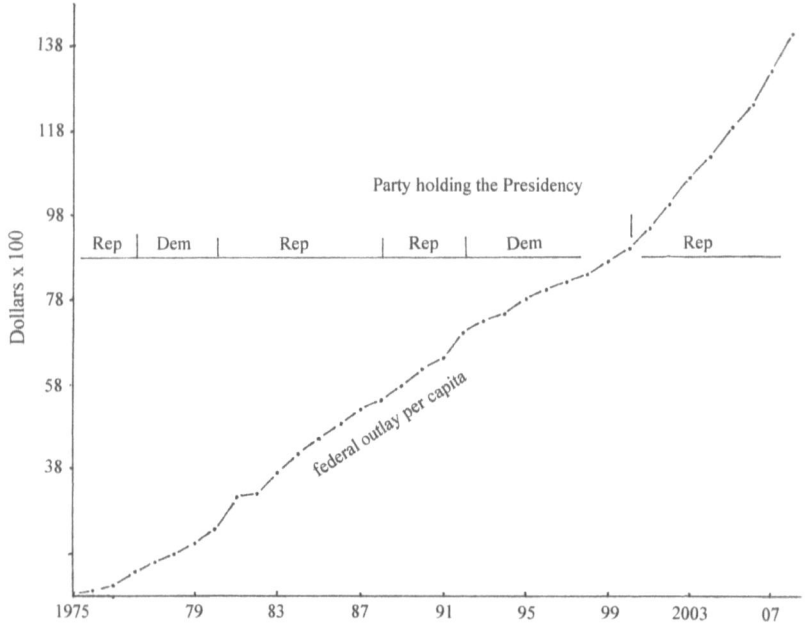

Graph 2   Inflation-adjusted federal expenditures, *per capita* from 1974 – 2008. Data from the "Economic Report of the President" 2011, Tables B-83 and B-31.

Another identifiable factor increasing costs is advancing technical sophistication. Computers, cars, radios, refrigerators, watches, cell phones, games etc. become more useful, complex, and expensive each year. Nowhere are these advances in complexity more dramatic and costly to taxpayers than those for military preparedness and health care.

It is highly probable that much of the increasing costs of governance per person are simply due to increasing complexity in all phases of life: ensuring the safety, legality, and effectiveness of commercial services and products through enforcement of laws.

In the financial world, the vehicles of profit are increasingly numerous and complex instruments that allow betting on a wide range of economic variables: security prices, currencies, commodity prices, interest rates, home prices, credit worthiness, and a bewildering array of financial derivatives based on these and other market variables.

National commissions and offices charged with understanding and regulating this world of speculation are large, expensive, and growing. Unfortunately, they haven't yet had the resources to keep ahead of financial innovations that can create profit for professionals but pose dangers for the public and the economy because of the enormous amounts of money involved. Case in point is the 2007-08 mortgage fiasco, a financial meltdown that triggered the ensuing Great Recession of 2008.

In the sciences and engineering, advances have unleashed a torrent of non-natural and manufactured products onto world markets and the environment. The Food and Drug Administration has had to establish increasingly numerous and sophisticated analytical laboratories both at home and abroad to detect dangerous, toxic, environmentally detrimental, and non-effective products. Medical science and practice continually introduce new therapies, tests, procedures, and drugs which must be assessed for efficacy and safety before entering a market of consumers who benefit but don't understand the health dangers involved.

The American Chemical Society as of 1/20/2014 has registered over fifty million unique chemicals. And chemists are seeking registration of new chemicals at an unbelievable pace. And this registration list doesn't include all proprietary substances created and used in commercial processing. Most of the new chemicals in this gargantuan torrent have never been tested for toxicity to living organisms or danger to the environment.

Some of us remember the tragedy of thalidomide, a marketed treatment for nausea in pregnant women which eventually was found to cause terrible birth abnormalities. Often it takes years to realize the environmental danger that a substance poses. Another case in point was the long-delayed discovery of the effects of DDT on bird and other animal populations. Local bird populations were wiped out before all of the effects of DDT became known.

National defense now involves a bewildering assortment of weapons and services unknown even a decade ago. Keeping up is not cheap. The *Washington Post* reported that defense budgets increased 88 percent between 1997 and 2011. Our military expenditures are reported to have exceeded those of the next 13 largest countries of the world combined. Recent military interventions have been undertaken in Kuwait, Iraq, and Afghanistan, with costs in trillions of dollars *without legislated tax revenue increases to pay for them.*

National security faces both internal and foreign enemies whose capabilities range from single assassinations to strikes with weapons of heavy destruction. A whole new Homeland Security Department was created in response. It now consists of more than 20 agencies, a staff of hundreds of thousands, and an annual budget of more than $45 billion. Border patrols, anti-personnel fences, and new surveillance methods against illegal immigration are expensive and the need for them is increasing.

The Environmental Protection Agency must deal with air and water pollution from more complicated and extensive sources. Pollutions include debris and toxins in lakes, rivers, and oceans, safe containment of radioactivity, control of a wide array of chemicals, and the encroaching development and destruction of natural habitats that animals and plants need for survival. Natural disasters of water, wind, and fire increase as the Earth warms.

Resources of water are being stretched as mountain snow packs, glaciers, and subterranean water sources become over-exploited and diminished. But the need for water keeps increasing.

More animal populations face extinction every day. The Bureau of Land Management has claimed too few resources to even accurately and efficiently ascertain whether federal and Indian resources are properly protected or whether federal and Indian mineral resources are at risk of being extracted without agency approval and land owner compensation. These short-comings are from a report of the Government Accountability Office, mentioned in regard to rapidly increasing natural gas extraction operations called fracking.

Federal agencies come into being to manage whole new worlds of cyber defense, health care advances, and communication technologies. The list goes on as investments in science and engineering continually make possible ever more labor-saving, life-saving, protective — and expensive — products.

Unfortunately, new products and programs invite unscrupulous scams aimed at a public mostly incapable of understanding the dangers or efficacy of technically sophisticated commercial offerings. The cost of government oversight and protection against all kinds of commercial fraud correspondingly increases as new and more complex products appear in the markets.

Can we test the idea that social complexity is a major driver of government cost increases? No, but there is a clue. The operations of the federal government are encoded in laws developed and enforced through time. This blueprint of government activity resides in a body of federal laws and regulations called *The Code of Laws of the United States* ("The Code"). The *Political Calculation* blog reported that in 1939 the complete "Code" contained 504 pages and since has grown steadily at an average rate of 3.28% per year. By 2006, the last year reported, The Code was over 200,000 pages and 42 million words. Is there growth and increasing complexity of government service, protection, and oversight? So it would seem.

Trying to foresee and prevent unscrupulous use of products, services, and laws is a gigantic task with every citizen, organization, and the opposing political party only too ready to heap condemnation on a government that fails to certify and achieve thorough legality, safety, and efficacy.

In considering this growth of laws and the associated implementation and enforcement of them, it is well to remember that every law passed is a congressionally-tested response to documented needs of people, businesses, institutions, and governments. And most of the regulations associated with a law are included to prevent people from exploiting it for personal profit. Mr. Norquist and other less extreme political operatives seem unaware that there are necessary costs of doing business and that cutting those costs is as bad for government as it is for business.

GOVERNMENT REGULATIONS IN THE OPERATIONS OF A FREE-MARKET ECONOMY

8

Regulatory irritations required for compliance with government laws include extensive efforts to prevent fraud and theft. Human ingenuity in circumventing laws is great and so are the regulations attempting to prevent it. We need to blow off steam about regulatory irritations but also need to look into a mirror for the full picture.

The trouble with laws, especially those that might cost us money or time, is that we humans are very good at finding ways to circumvent their intent for personal advantage. Our ingenuity in getting around laws is the reason that laws are loaded with provisions and regulations: efforts to ensure that they are followed.

The number or amount of government regulations, however, has become staggering. Cass R. Sunstein, former head of the *White House Office of Information and Regulatory Affairs* published a calculation in 2013 of the number of hours Americans spend on government-required paperwork. Hold your breath. It turned out to be 9.14 billion hours per year! At a minimal cost of ten dollars an hour, the cost in money would be $90 billion. And this figure doesn't begin to capture the frustration and annoyance of grappling with all those forms. In the last chapter we learned that the cost of government per person was going up faster than inflation and increases in population. Increasing regulatory requirements, and their enforcement, has to be a major part of that increasing cost.

Of the government departments whose services require regulations, the Treasury Department is the national champion, requiring some 74 percent of total regulatory work. Most of the Treasury regulations and requirements come through the Internal Revenue Service which is burdened by complicated tax laws, made and continuously fine-tuned by Congress.

The only good news in the regulatory department is that the problem is at least recognized. That *White House Office of Information and Regulatory Affairs* oversees the *Paperwork Reduction Acts of 1980 and 1995.* This agency does not make the news but works quietly over the years to eliminate unnecessary regulatory requirements. In their work, modest ways to reduce the time and expense involved have been tried, proposed, and sometimes adopted. Needless to say, their work needs support and perhaps some enforcement authority from both parties in Congress.

Brokers and analysts working inside financial institutions sometimes use private information, not available to the general public, making profitable trades in financial markets for themselves and preferred clients. This practice, called insider trading, is illegal. Back in 1884 the *Insider Trading Sanctions Act* was passed to eliminate it. Enforcement and oversight agencies have had their hands full in trying to detect and prosecute such behavior through courts of law. The act and numberless subsequent legislative efforts still are not completely successful in stopping this threat to market credibility. Efforts to eliminate or penalize insider trading continue at great tax-payer expense.

Misleading information was used by banks and investment

firms in selling securities to the public. The government responded with the *Securities Act of 1933*. It required government oversight (reams of verifying paperwork) of the information published by brokers to explain and sell their financial products.

John D. Rockefeller's Standard Oil Company and J.P.Morgan's United States Steel Corporation were near monopolies in the late 1800's, ruthlessly squeezing out smaller competitors. *The Sherman Antitrust Act of 1890* and many subsequent laws and federal actions have come into being to outlaw such restraints on the competition that a free market economy requires. We will have more to say later about current mergers and acquisitions of businesses that are eroding market competition that is necessary for keeping prices down.

Bankers and investors, seeking greater profits in financial markets, misread market fundamentals and risk factors, causing a catastrophic financial meltdown in 1929. This plunged the U.S. economy into the Great Depression of the 1930's. To prevent it from happening again, the *Glass-Steagal Act of 1933* was enacted, which among many things, forbad commercial banks from risking depositors' money in financial speculations. Commercial banking was required to be in separate institutions from stock brokerages.

Long and intense pressure from banks finally led to the act's cancellation in 1999. A persuasive argument used by the banks to achieve this was how risk factors could now be more accurately assessed and controlled through new risk-hedging techniques. The cancellation of the law in 1999 was the crucial factor in allowing both banks and high rolling investors to achieve unusually high profits leading up to the 2008 financial meltdown.

Laborers often have been subjected to dangerous or unsanitary conditions by companies wanting to cut production costs. Between 1900 and 1910, for example, mining fatalities exceeded 2,000 a year. In direct response, Congress established the *Bureau of Mines* and later the *Mining Enforcement and Safety*

Administration Act in 1978. Today the Department of Labor houses the *Occupational Safety and Health Administration* (OSHA) which enforces the many laws and regulations designed to protect workers from unsafe or unhealthy working conditions imposed by companies seeking ever lower production costs in competitive markets.

A Stanberry Advisory report in 2011, "Corporate Corruption and the Securities and Exchange Commission," summarized examples of financial fraud by some of our biggest institutions. In the Enron scandal, for example, it reported that the SEC watchdog had investigated and concluded that Citigroup and J.P. Morgan knowingly aided Enron Corporation in executing deceptive accounting and illegal transactions.

Interestingly, few criminal prosecutions have been documented, although in this Advisory Report there were nine SEC charges of fraud and illegal activity against these big banking corporations. Every year several accusations have been surfacing against the big Wall Street banks. As a result we will take a closer look at the nature of such activities in a later chapter.

These examples make the point that in the drumbeat of regulatory accusations against businesses and individuals we see why, in the first place, government laws are developed: to meet the obligations of service to, and protection of, its citizens. These laws and regulations often contain hundreds of pages of details to prevent illegal attempts to use them for personal gain. The oversight and implementation of laws, new and old, have required the creation of many costly bureaus, commissions, and oversight bodies. Much, and likely most, of the growing size and expense of the federal government is directly related to creation and enforcement of these laws.

Since laws, regulations, and the increasing complexity of our society are significant factors in increasing federal expenditures, we will take a historical glance at the origin of a few important regulatory laws. Our historical glance will demonstrate that laws and regulations most often arise as direct responses to various kinds of business fraud, tax shenanigans, or the many other ways we law-abiding citizens of this great nation seek to maximize our assets with the minimum amount of time and trouble.

FINANCIAL ASSETS IN THE U.S. ECONOMY

9

Financial speculation is necessary for the pricing of products and services and the initiation, expansion, and innovation of businesses. Such speculations have become well expanded beyond their usefulness in the productive economy. These excessive speculations have enriched investors but done little or nothing for the productive, job-supplying goods and services economy.

M oney used for making more money, working capital, is the life blood of the economy. It is money invested in the financing, creation, and sale of goods and services. It also is the money invested in the jobs whose wages drive the economy through consumption of those goods and services.

The goods and services sectors are the productive foundation of our economy. These are the sectors which employ the vast majority of American workers. The financial sectors also have a crucial role, providing the money for development of businesses as well as for private financing of big ticket items like cars and homes for consumers. Financial businesses create profits though lending, speculative investments, management of financial investments, and sales of insurance or lease of real estate. There are fundamental differences, however, between goods and services businesses and financial businesses.

Financial sectors have a pattern of growth that has deviated from those of the goods and services. Between 1945 and the 1970's, profits produced by the financial sectors grew at about the same rate as profits produced in goods and services. These two great parts of our economy were closely linked through cooperative business interactions.

After the late 1970's, however, more types of profit-seeking financial speculations were introduced that had little or nothing to do with goods and services businesses. Increasing amounts of working capital were invested in financial speculations, motivated by lower tax rates on their profits. By 2001, profits of the financial sectors, which employed relatively few American workers, were close to half of all U.S. corporate profits.

In 2011 the Department of Labor reported that 6.8 percent of American workers were employed in financial sectors and that percentage was trending downward. Average wages of non-supervisory workers in financial services were 74 percent higher than the average non-supervisory wages in goods and services. Compensations of executives in financial firms also were extraordinarily high.

The Wall Street Journal reported in 2010 that compensation and benefits of manager-level employees in the 25 largest publically owned financial firms was $135 billion, and that was 5.7 percent greater than the year before. Just the managers of the top 25 hedge funds took home $22.02 billion that year. Despite unusually rich rewards for their skills, however, the sector accounted for less than ten percent of value added in the U.S. economy.

Forbes Magazine, listing the world's billionaires in 2012, noted that of the 425 U.S. billionaires, 101 of them were listed as having acquired their fortunes in financial sectors while the others undoubtedly supplemented their earned incomes with unearned financial income. The U.S. technology sector, which is driving much of new investment and growth in goods and services, was a poor second with only 51 billionaires.

According to a report in the New York Times, about one third of financial sector profits come from fees charged for money management, with profits from lending, leasing, and various kinds of speculations making up the other two-thirds. And it seems likely that the rapid increase in financial sector profits since the 1970's is helped by the continuing introduction of profitable speculative instruments. Examples include home mortgages bundled into saleable securities and derivative innovations of bewildering complexity and variety based on real market variables and risks. Much of the increase of profits in financial sectors is due to increasing amounts of U.S. working capital, earned in goods and services but diverted into financial speculations.

Americans with discretionary money in excess of living requirements, invest mostly in financial equities that constitute a secondary, unearned income. Such investments don't buy goods and services, sales of which are what sustain the goods and services economy. Instead, those investments draw income from rent, interest, dividends, and growth in value of securities — as well as potential profits from bets on such things as international currency exchange rates or other market variations.

According to an article in the New York Times' Business section, 1/12/14, the amount of money in the financial sectors is immense: $53 trillion in 2013. That amount of money is three times as much as the national debt of 2013 and more than three times the size of total government revenue of 2013. So where does all this working capital, invested in financial securities and speculations, go?

Some is invested in shares of company stock or bonds that support public or private enterprise. Such investments support prime elements of the U.S. economy.

Far smaller amounts are invested in beginning businesses

or business ideas that are high risk, high return ventures that are highly valuable to our evolving economy. Of limited use in the general economy are billions of dollars invested in gold, high end art, or other valuables which act to conserve capital and reap benefit from potential future increases in price. Of no help to the economy are the trillions of dollars of profits held in offshore investment centers by individuals and companies where their trillions generate interest which is available for increasing personal wealth or business investment abroad but *un*available for employment of the wage-earners or business investment in their home economy or for tax support of their government.

While most of the upper half of American households have some discretionary capital for investment in financial assets, the lower half, consisting overwhelmingly of workers in goods and services, seldom have discretionary capital beyond retirement program contributions. Especially since the 1980's, that lower half of American earners have not been able to participate in the increases in productivity and profits provided by the expanding economy. This bottom half, not having discretionary capital to invest, have seen their working wages stagnate or decrease through inflation. This does much to account for increasing levels of poverty and the unhealthy inequality of income and wealth among Americans.

This leaving behind of half of Americans, this phenomenon of unequal distribution of income and wealth, has been thoroughly described and given an international and historical perspective in Thomas Piketty's book mentioned in the Introduction and in the General References at the end. Because of the enormous importance of this highly unequal distribution of income and wealth in America's capitalistic society, we will return to it in later chapters.

SUCCESSES AND DANGERS IN U.S. MEGABANK OPERATIONS

10

Financial institutions are essential in our free-market economy but the gigantic size of our largest banks and the magnitude of their speculations pose a potential, and unnecessary, danger to the nation and its economy.

F inancial institutions are integral to capitalist economies to which most of the developed nations of the world are now committed. Those economies operate in many variations, mostly involving the degree of help and/or control their governments exercise over their markets and financial institutions.

In this chapter I will continue highlighting contrasts between the financial sectors and the goods and services sectors of the U.S. economy. In doing so, I will describe aspects of financial institutions which are disproportionately large and will dwell in some detail on borrowing risks and potential systemic danger. In these discussions, it will become ever more evident what is causing the increasing degree of income and wealth disparity in American households.

On some of these subjects, the narrative is highly critical of some aspects of financial institutions. In fact, however, most financial institutions are performing necessary services in American communities and we could not do without them or the many skilled professionals working there. But we will see that too much American capital is being withdrawn into financial sectors when goods and services sectors are where the jobs and productive investments and innovations are needed.

The historian and commentator, Kevin Phillips, has pointed out a recurring pattern in past world commercial empires. Early direct-market systems required little or no financial services. With the settling down into communities, however, came more complex buying and selling and with it the rise of larger and more productive businesses that needed financial help for establishment and growth. These early systems left a rich heritage of human attitudes and laws concerning commerce, much of which is still with us embedded in current commercial laws.

During the industrial revolution, as advancing productivity and complexity created more requirements for investment capital, banking and investment services increased in importance. In this evolution, Mr. Phillips noticed an interesting thing: high degrees of financial speculation on commercial activities were associated with the final decline of Hapsburg Spain in the 16th century, the Dutch trading empire of the 18th, and the British empire of the 19th century. In each case, the demise of these world empires was marked by the increasing amounts of capital committed to financial speculative investment.

Financial speculation is based on risk. Lenders and speculators weigh the risk of a loan or an investment against possible returns. In general, the higher the potential return, the greater the risk. As financial players accumulate experience and devise methods of assessing and mitigating risk, increasing confidence motivates them toward the higher rewards gained through greater risk.

As long as betting failures occur in manageable amounts, little damage is done to the greater economy. It is the accumulation of vast amounts of investment capital by large banks and other investment cooperatives where bets reach a magnitude where failure not only threatens lenders and speculators but, through herd panic phenomena, whole financial systems.

Very large financial disasters like those of 1929 and 2008 cause widespread and prolonged economic distress for millions of people, institutions, and nations. Such melt-downs illustrate just how much damage the failure of large, functionally inter-connected financial institutions can cause to the economies on which we all depend.

Before the abolition of fixed international exchange rates at Bretton Woods, most financial activity was mediated by smaller commercial banks where loans were made to people and busi-nesses using money from client's savings deposits. Bank profits came from interest on their loans and fees for their services. Although fairly boring work by the standards of the fast-break-ing investment positions taken today with huge amounts, smaller commercial bankers still operate and live in the best circles of their communities with high social standing. Their work is a necessary, rewarding, and demanding calling.

When international exchange rates were allowed to float in 1971 and the value of the dollar was uncoupled from the price of gold, national currencies began to fluctuate in relative value and speculation on future exchange rates took off. U.S. speculation on currency exchange rates in 1970 amounted to $110.8 billion. Seven years later, the Federal Reserve Bank of New York found that foreign exchange speculations had increased to about $1.2 trillion a year, an increase of about 11 times.

The rapid growth in recent years of financial sectors in gen-eral can be seen in their growth as a percent of America's GDP. Harvard economists David Scharfstein and Robin Greenwood found the financial industry had grown from 2.8% of GDP in 1950 to 8.3% in 2006, almost a 200 percent increase.

High speed investment transactions have added a new dimen-sion to financial speculations. Computer-driven investments, based on mathematically derived algorithms and operating in split seconds, have become wide-spread. This kind of high-speed transaction depends on reactions to buy or sell orders in a particular market. Large orders or sales will cause a transitory change of price in a manner that can be anticipated and exploited for a quick profit.

Because higher profits can be realized in financial speculations than in lending, the incentives are high for betting and for cutting regulatory corners to achieve those profits. With such strong incentives there should be no surprise at a continuous drumbeat of accusations of illegal shenanigans against investment banks and other investment consortiums by U.S. financial oversight bodies such at the *Securities and Exchange Commission* (SEC) and the *Consumer Financial Protection Bureau (*CFPB). A few examples will give an indication of the varied nature of illegal actions that have attracted attention by these regulatory agencies.

In 2003 Citigroup settled for $400 million for falsified research findings.

In 2010 Goldman Sachs paid $550 million to settle allegations of sale of fraudulently advertised mortgage securities.

In 2013 the JP Morgan Chase Bank was found guilty of selling mortgages of substandard underwriting quality to unsuspecting investors. The bank settled for $13 billion and admission of guilt.

From the New York Times (4/12/2000) a few examples from their "Financial Scandal Scoreboard" article.

* Peregrine Financial Group, Cedar Falls, Iowa: illegally using depositors' money.
* MF Global: $1.6 billion gone missing.
* HSBC Bank: did business with an institution doing money laundering for drug traffickers.
* Capital One: deceptively marketing needless add-on products to financial instruments.

The list goes on, but the amounts of money borrowed to make some speculations are so large, compared with the amount of assets covering those loans and bets, that real danger exists in the U.S. and global financial systems. This is precisely what led to the mortgage crisis of 2007.

Financial institutions receive public criticism about fees charged for their services. Observers have noted a relative dearth of competition in management fees charged by financial managers when compared to professional services in other sectors of the economy. Fees for financial services follow generally-accepted percentage guidelines throughout the industry. In goods and services sectors, providers of services *compete* for business with fees based on the kind and reputed quality of their services. Think of medicine, law, science, sports, art, education, and political office for examples.

The scope and volume of financial speculations have been enormously expanded by the invention and use of derivatives. These investment instruments include contracts bought from banks by speculators who bet on price or other market aspects of real market variations such as interest rates, currency exchange rates, commodity price changes, credit standing, equity prices etc. In the event of a borrower's default on a bet, the contract would require the bank to repay the lender's full loan.

As hedges against risk, such derivatives have insurance value for lenders. They also produce much profit for the few big banks that control most of this business. The profits from the contracts must be substantial because those contracting banks vigorously defend their derivative business against other banks and insurance institutions.

One thing about derivative markets stands out: investment banks are using derivative instruments for their own speculative betting — as well as for the risk-hedging contracts with other lenders mentioned above. It is the amounts of money involved in these contracts and speculations that can create risk for the banks, for the lenders they have covered, and potentially the financial system. To give some idea of the risk these large banks undertake, we can ask how much of their risk in dollars is covered by their assets in dollars. A bank's risk comes from its own speculations and from derivative contracts the banks have undertaken to cover in case of a borrower's default.

A 2011 report from the Office of the Comptroller of the Currency (OCC) showed that the five biggest banks in the U.S. held 96 percent of *known* derivative contracts and 96 percent of that risk. As of June, 2012, OCC reported on the notional amount, the estimated market value of the real market entities underlying these derivative contracts in the U.S.

In that year the notional value of those U.S. contracts totaled about $222 trillion. That was 16 times more than the entire U.S. GDP of 2012! Using published figures from the OCC for 2012, J.P. Morgan Bank was potentially liable for a total risk of $69.2 trillion worth of loans with covering assets that were only 2.6 percent of that amount in dollars. Citibank had potential liabilities of $52.1 trillion with total assets of 2.6 percent of that amount. Bank of America had potential liabilities of $44.4 trillion with total assets of 3.2 percent of that amount. Goldman Sachs' had potential liabilities of $41.8 trillion with total assets amounting to 0.3 percent of that amount.

If derivative contract defaults exceed their available capital through some combination of financial failure and a more general investor panic, banks themselves face default. Because of the gigantic amounts of money involved, these derivative contracts pose a risk that well-known investor, Warren Buffet, warned about back in 2003. He noted that derivatives were highly complex contracts that are potential "financial weapons of mass destruction."

So we see possible danger in these highly profitable financial markets. First, because derivative markets are efficient in transaction costs and for borrowing of capital, they encourage increasing market speculation while risk can seemingly be hedged by derivative contracts. Second, the variety and complexity of derivative contracts make it more possible to exploit their complexity to practice fraud and manipulation to get around regulations and avoid taxes. Third, new ways to shift credit risk in over-the-counter derivative contracts can be devised which are not subject to mandated requirements for loan-covering assets. Such evasions lead to greater aggregate risk. We saw an example of that risk in the four mega banks quoted above whose total assets cover only two to three percent of their contractual obligations.

In summary, we note that the financial sectors have been hugely successful in creating profits for managers, investors, and stock-holders. Those profits amount to a disproportionate share of the working capital available to the U.S. economy. This accumulation has accelerated since the mid-1990s as new forms of investments are invented and ever larger amounts of capital transferred from goods and services sectors into financial speculations.

The financial sectors enjoy high, relatively non-competitive management and transaction fees. Motivated by higher returns on more risky, complex investments, some investors have been shown to resort to illegal manipulations of the system.

Some claim with reason that the sheer size and complexity of these huge investment banks make it impossible for top executives to maintain effective control or accept responsibility for what employees of the corporation do with corporate money. Currently, it is seldom that a government oversight body detects and proves illegal activity but be able to prosecute the responsible individual. Do these institutions have any legal responsibility for what individuals do under their corporate protection? Or do the fines imposed just represent a sustainable cost of doing high-profit business with no personal culpability?

THE ACCUMULATION OF MOST OF AMERICA'S FINANCIAL ASSETS BY A SMALL MINORITY OF AMERICANS

11

The wealth in possession of top-earning U.S. households includes a very high proportion of the nation's financial assets, much of it earned in goods and services but diverted into wealth-enhancing financial speculations. How does this accumulation of financial assets happen?

N ot all Americans know just how successful our wealthy business elite have become in the making and accumulation of money. It is a fascinating story, highlighted by Republican insistence on reducing national debt by almost any mechanism *except* increasing tax revenues from very wealthy people.

After about 1973, wages for American workers have stagnated with little real growth. As families tried to maintain their life styles, more wives and mothers entered the work force. Efforts of families to sustain familiar amenities resulted in more borrowing. Associated with tightening household budgets, tensions over finances undoubtedly afflicted more families: increasing divorce rates; more poor or delinquent children in public schools; teachers struggling to maintain educational standards with less help from working parents.

The economy, however, has grown robustly since 1973. The GDP increased 223% from 1973 to 2012. From this increasing economic activity came increased profits. Where did they go?

Studies reported by G. William Domhoff of the University of California at Santa Cruz show where that income went from 1981 to 2007. His report showed that the top one percent of U.S. earners held 25 percent of U.S. wealth in 1981 at the end of President Carter's administration. By 2007 their wealth had reached 35 percent of the U.S. total. Much of this had been invested in financial assets because by 2007 this top one percent held half of all U.S. financial assets.

The accumulation of the nation's wealth by the top one percent is reflected also in data on incomes, reported by Emmanuel Saez, an economist at the University of California, Berkeley. From 1993 to 2006 the incomes of the top one percent of Americans increased on average 5.7 percent a year while the incomes of the bottom 99% of Americans grew an average of 1.1 percent a year. These numbers tell us that the top one percent captured about half of the growth in incomes from 1993 to 2006!

In a separate analysis, the Congressional Budget Office looked at American incomes after taxes and adjustment for inflation in the period 1979 to 2007. That report showed that average income for the top one percent increased 275 percent; income for the top 20 percent increased 65 percent while those in the bottom 20 percent grew only 18 percent in those 28 years.

With so much of the profits generated by a growing economy going to top earners, we might ask how all that income was used. Domhoff found that the top 1 percent in 2007 had invested the discretionary part of their incomes in a high proportion of U.S. financial assets: 61 percent of all U.S. securities and 38 percent of U.S. mutual funds. This tells us that the earned incomes of top earners provide a great deal of discretionary money above what their life styles demand and which they can invest in wealth-enhancing financial speculations.

This secondary unearned income, well invested, grows as an addition to the earned incomes from their business activities. The accumulation of capital in their possession would not have been nearly as rapid without their financial investments whose return on investments contributed to the increase of their wealth. In growing economies, the more discretionary money you have and invest the faster your wealth increases, especially when taxes on such unearned income are lower than on earned income.

Higher monetary rewards for higher ability are a natural result of the spectrum of human capabilities, something we all understand and respect. But as more and more of a nation's available capital ends up in the hands of the most able money makers, some upper limit of wealth of those top earners is passed when the percent of a nation's financial assets, possessed by the few, begins to have negative effects on the other money earners.

As of this writing, the amount of American capital held by the top few percent of Americans has accumulated to levels not seen since the roaring 20's, just before the market crash of 1929. It is at these levels that a concept of *excessive* wealth can arise, a concept that considers the well-being of the vast majority a priority over the highly unusual well-being of a few.

The large accumulation of national capital at the top gives these wealthy individuals more than opulent life styles. It also gives them enormous political power in U.S. governments at all levels. That political power is used vigorously to defend and conserve, through the nation's laws, the origins and taxation of their wealth.

It seems obvious that the U.S. economy, businesses,

government, and the well-being of the nation as a whole, would benefit if some part of the financial assets sequestered in the financial speculations of the very wealthy were redistributed more widely to American workers. Such an action would create more goods and service consumption, allowing more job creation and enabling increases in businesses income and profit.

The contested point in this 'spread-more-of-the-wealth' assertion is the Republican claim that accumulation of wealth at the top is essential for the business investments that enable our economy to grow (trickling down assets). If this assertion is true, we might inquire how such massive amounts of capital accumulated by top households gets diverted from goods and service sectors into unearned profits from their financial holdings.

A look at the compensation of top earners reveals a lot. The top executives of big companies, the CEO's, are paid earned salaries like other workers. But, in addition, their Boards of Directors (whose appointment to their Boards the CEO's usually have a dominant voice) often reward their work with cash bonuses, stock awards, stock options, and other perquisites. These motivation bonuses come out of before-tax profits rather than as profit to company stockholders or to company investments in research and development.

The compensations of top U.S. executives, relative to what their employees make, are higher than in other developed countries. A report by Steven McDonnell, published in the *Houston Chronicle*, found the average CEO compensation in U.S. companies to be 400-500 times more than the median salary of their employees. In contrast, top executives in the UK average 22 times as much, in France 15 times, and in Germany 12 times as much as the median salary of their employees. This study included companies of many sizes.

Another comparison of top level executive compensations at very large U.S. and European corporations was undertaken by *Pedersen and Partners* for the year 2012. They found that when total compensations were compared, U.S. CEO's received on average 23% more than their European counterparts, the difference being mostly in stock options to the Americans. The authors of this study concluded that "not only are the top executives of large companies granted much higher compensation packages than most of their lower managers and employees, their compensations also have increased twice as fast in both short and long term." So CEO's of big companies in the U.S. get unusually high compensation in comparison with those of other developed nations.

In another study of compensations, The New York Times in June of 2013 reported the compensations of the top executives of the 200 biggest U.S. corporations for 2012. At the top of this list was Lawrence J. Ellison of the Oracle Company who took home over $96 million that year. This was more than double what he made the year before. Just the CEO's of those biggest 200 companies received a total of about $3.5 billion in compensation in 2012. The same report listed the combined personal wealth of those 200 executives at over $67 billion. (Wealth = financial assets plus tangible wealth such as buildings, machinery etc.)

These figures are representative for a number of the top one percent of wealthy households of the U.S. The compensations of executives and lower managers of 25 Wall St. financial firms plus the compensations of CEO's of the 200 big corporations, added up to $139 billion in that year. To give a government perspective of this amount of money, it is more than the combined discretionary budgets ($133 billion) of the federal Department of Education, the National Science Foundation (funding much U.S. scientific research), and the large Department of Homeland Security.

This information makes the point that top executives of large corporations make a lot of money in comparison to top executives in other developed countries. Most of the capital gained through these yearly compensations, far beyond what even the best life styles can demand, goes into securities, valuables, or speculations of one kind or another to increase or conserve that wealth.

Much of this wealth, earned in the U.S. economy, is sequestered abroad in 'discrete' accounts. Publicized in February 2014 was a U.S. Senate bipartisan probe into secret accounts held in the Swiss banking giant Credit Suisse. The probe revealed that accounts of 22,000 wealthy Americans totaled $12 billion in this one bank. The owners of these accounts were not identified and, although the money was earned by Americans, the owners paid no U.S. tax on it for the seven years examined by the probe.

Presidential candidate in 1992, Ross Perot, coined a term, "a giant sucking sound," to describe what he predicted would be the sound of American jobs leaving the U.S. for near-by countries because of the North American Free Trade Pact. It could equally be used to describe the flow of earned money, made through productive work in the U.S. economy, into lower-taxed financial investments and tax shelters here and abroad.

It is easy to see that this diversion of money is bad for the country because of its removal from the productive goods and services economy where the jobs are and where the wages support the U.S. economy and its businesses. We shall return to this point when considering the Republican insistence that this accumulation of capital is essential for the business investments that expand the economy and create jobs.

THE DISTRIBUTION OF FINANCIAL ASSETS IN THE U.S. ECONOMY

12

Financial assets in the U.S. are not unlimited and a high proportion are in possession of the top few percent of American households. Here, we look at the magnitude of this accumulation and explore a theoretical scenario to see what might happen if some of that capital were made available for stimulating the economy and increasing business activity, thus generating more and better jobs for American workers and more profit for businesses.

I n early September, 2014, The Federal Reserve issued its triennial *Survey of Consumer Finances,* a comprehensive source of data on the financial assets of Americans. The report revealed a yawning gulf between what the top few percent of households received from the expanding American economy and what the bottom 90+ percent were getting.

During the years 2010 to 2013 the U.S. economy grew robustly, increasing wealth and financial assets. For the most affluent ten percent of American families, their average income rose by ten percent and their estimated wealth by two percent to an average of $3.3 million per household in those three years. For the lower 90 percent, the average income was constant or falling. Average income for the lowest 20 percent fell by 8 percent with their average wealth decreasing 21 percent! These estimates of wealth included financial assets as well as tangible assets such as houses, cars, and computer systems.

This accumulation of national assets at the top is characteristic for all capitalistic nations in varying degrees. The Federal Reserve report documented the size of this income and wealth gap in the U.S. The top 3 percent of American families collected 31.4 percent of total American *income* by 2010 and it was fluctuating around 30.5 percent in 2013. In terms of family *wealth*, the top 3 percent of families possessed 44.8 percent of total American wealth in 1989, 51.8 percent in 2007, and 54.4 percent by 2013.

The Fed, in that report, also reported a decline in the number of Americans who had discretionary income that could be invested for secondary, unearned income. In 2010, 15.1 percent of American families directly owned stock. By 2013 that number had fallen to 13.8 percent. This report informs us that the accumulation of American wealth by a relatively small elite has reached a very high level, and that the percentage of people with enough discretionary capital for financial investment is decreasing.

Probably the most intransigent of the conflicts between congressional Democrats and Republicans in recent years has centered on the national debt, an issue brought to high public consciousness by Republican politicians. Although presently at an uncomfortable level, debt at some level has always been with us as a percent of GDP.

Public rhetoric and policy pronouncements from the political right assert that taxation is high and government too big. This assertion promotes the idea that current levels of government services, especially social services such as health care, are high and unsustainable for our GDP 'income'. The political right will not allow raising taxes on the wealthy, claiming that their wealth is needed for business investment, economic expansion, and more jobs.

The political left seems willing to explore some cuts in social services but looks for more tax revenue from the top of the wealth spectrum to mitigate the negative human impact of those cuts. In addition, the left promotes the use of public money for creating jobs that stimulate the economy while maintaining the nation's infrastructure and environment. This is what Roosevelt did with his CCC and WPA programs in the 1930's.

The United States is more than a huge national market. In close partnership, the U.S. government and its business communities have indeed created the world's greatest national economy. But for U.S. citizens, in either private or public work, it also is their nation: a place to receive an education and acquire a sense of national history, pride, and values. It is a familiar place for establishing identities within families and communities. It is a bulwark that safeguards its citizens in this overpopulated, violently contending world of different ideologies and cultures. Yet, seldom have our national identity and pride been more compromised by partisan strife that paralyzes the government over issues of government size and tax policies that support its many services.

At this point in time with strife and violence spreading around the world, a crucial question must be asked. Does our government actually have sufficient economic power to maintain adequate jobs and services for its citizens and the traditional American dream of betterment for their children – or must we now learn to live with fewer government amenities and a lesser dream?

Before the late 1970's, federal expenditures paralleled economic output at around 16 -18 percent of GDP while high federal debt, remaining after World War II, was slowly decreased to comfortable levels. Yearly increases in federal expenses always occur. This is caused by increases in population, inflation, new laws, natural catastrophes, international involvements etc. In the 1970's, however, federal expenditures began to increase significantly faster than GDP.

As detailed in a previous chapter, federal deficits began to balloon when President Reagan initiated his experiment of lowering income taxes to stimulate the economy. The hoped-for increase in tax revenue did not materialize and revenues were insufficient to offset increasing government spending. The national debt, as percent of GDP, increased still further under the same lowered taxation policies and the foreign war expenditures of the two Bush administrations.

These things are made clear by graphing statistical data (Graph 3 below). The two lines show yearly expenditures and revenues as *percent of GDP* (an approximation of our national income). An increase of top income tax to 39.6 percent, an economic internet technology boom, and a modest cut in federal expenditures during President Clinton's administration temporarily interrupted the increasing size of the deficit by producing revenues greater than expenditures for a few years. A sharp decrease in revenues is readily apparent after President G.W. Bush again cut taxes on top incomes. These top incomes produce a large share of tax revenue so cutting them again is associated with further increases in national debt.

Much public discussion of national debt is now framed by the sky-rocketing costs of health care. The impression fostered by conservative politicians is that if we get rid of *The Affordable Care Act* we would be further along on our way to deficit reduction. But the problem of deficit spending is far more long-term and complex than trying to reduce the cost of a long-needed national health program.

In 2012, the several government departments acting directly in the nation's defense (military, homeland security, non-military civil defense, and veterans' affairs) showed the greatest combined outlay of $899.726 billion. The Department of Health and Human Services was second at $848.056 billion. The costs of public health care are of real concern but still second to those associated with defending the nation against foreign aggressions with by far the greatest military in the world.

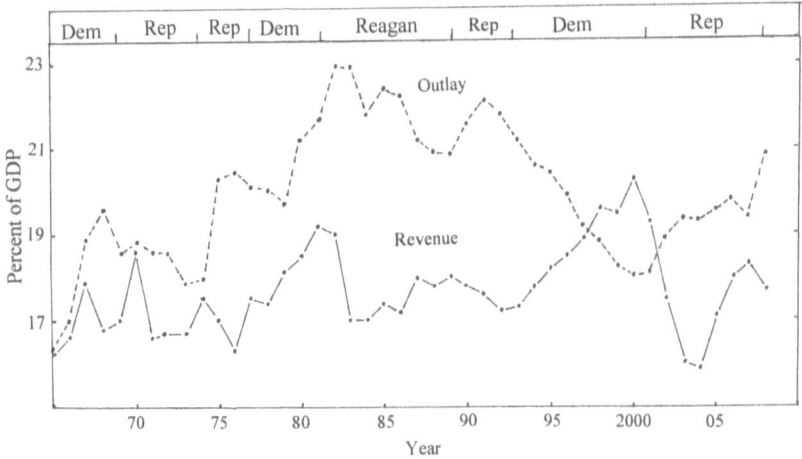

Graph 3   Federal outlays and revenue as percent of GDP, 1965 – 2009. Data from the Tax Policy Center, "Historical Federal Receipt and Outlay as Percent GDP."

I used Tables from a White House report to analyze increases in federal departmental expenditures from 1963 to 2007. The period selected was terminated at 2007 to eliminate the unusual, emergency expenditures necessitated by the financial crisis of 2008.

In Graph 4 below we see a period in time marked only by regular business cycles and oft-recurring extra departmental expenses. *Increases* in expenditures by the federal departments are expressed as multiples of their 1963 expenditures: doubling in size would register as 2 on the bottom scale. Increase of GDP is represented as a labeled vertical bar.

We see immediately that 10 of the 24 departments have increased more than the GDP. The average expenditures of all federal departments increased 23 times during those years while the GDP increased only 21 times. Individual administrative agencies showing the greatest increases were Executive Office of the President, Health and Human Services, Judicial Branch (including federal prisons), and Environmental Protection. Defense department costs have always been at or near the top of departmental expenditures so percent *increases*, tallied here, were not great.

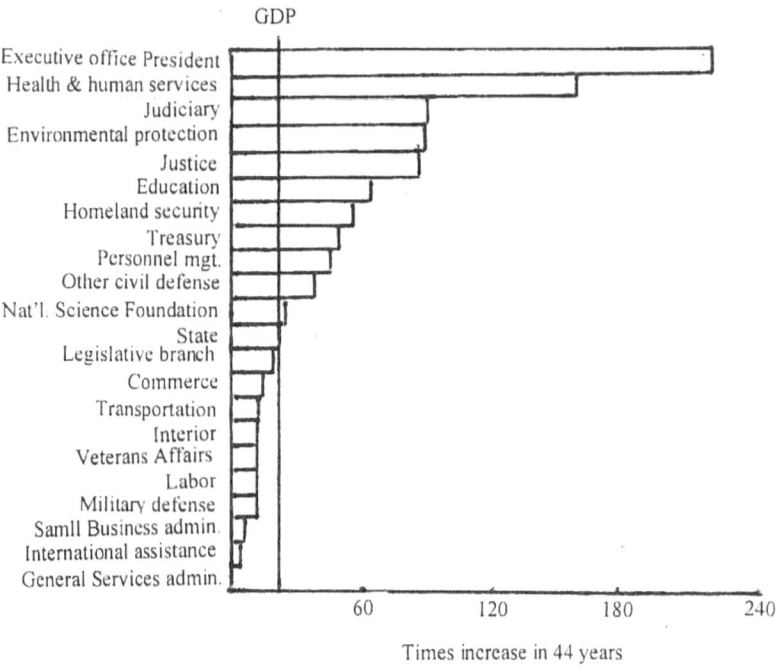

Graph 4   Increases in Federal department expenditures are shown as horizontal bars whose length is proportional to their times increase between 1963 and 2007. Data from a White House report wwww.whitehouse.gov/OMB/budget/historicals. Table 4.1

The Executive Office of the President showed the greatest increase, involving three Democratic and five Republican administrations. That Office had expenditures of $2,956 million in 2007. The sharp increases in Health and Human Services are no surprise but large increases in EPA and the Justice Department should be a clear warning that our environment and justice systems also are requiring much greater resources to meet mandated obligations.

Aside from the expenses of foreign wars, what accounts for accelerating increases in most other departments? In Chapter seven the increasing size and complexity of almost every aspect of American culture and government were pointed out. From personal every-day experience, it is easy for all of us to understand that life now is far more complex and costly than in the simpler days of 1963. Graph 4 gives us a better picture of where this complexity, size, and associated costs are coming from.

New increases in the national debt began during the Reagan administration in the 1980's. To get a better insight of what accounts for the increasing debt after President Reagan's lowered tax experiment, I again consulted the *Economic Report of the President, 2013*, for historical data between the years 1981, when Reagan took over, and 2012. The results are shown in Table 1.

Table 1

Budget Category	Percent Change 1981 - 2012
GDP	468.5% increase
Federal expenditures	518.1% increase
Federal revenues	372.2% increase

What Table 1 makes clear is that federal expenditures have increased faster than GDP while federal revenues have increased slower. The gap between expenditures and GDP during this period was exaggerated by the emergency expenditures of 2007 and 2008.

If this information shows anything, it is that since the introduction and use of low tax policies by President Reagan in the 1980's, the costs of government are not being met by tax revenues. Cases in point are recent news reports of large backlogs of service and under-funding at IRS, Border Security, Internal Revenue, Postal Services, Bureau of Land Management, and Veterans Hospitals.

Conservatives might counter that what these data show is increasing government costs due primarily to increasing inefficiency and/or bureaus and agencies coming into being that are redundant in action or whose costs could be reduced by more efficient private contractors.

I have to agree that public agencies, lacking competition in non-profit *servicing*, need to be critically evaluated and adjusted regularly. But having agreed to that, I also believe that profit-maximizing motivations in private enterprise need to be watched even more carefully, especially private companies using public money. Cheating the government or unsuspecting consumers is a well-known curse in the private commercial world, documented almost daily in news media.

Americans do not want a permanent underclass: homeless people under their bridges or their cities surrounded by shanty towns. But Americans probably agree on another thing too: In the long run, the costs of governing and maintaining a reasonably satisfied citizenry must be held within what our economy can sustainably provide.

A central question then is this: Given the national and global economic realities of today, does the U.S. economy produce sufficient profits to provide health and security for the vast majority of its citizens, at least at a level comparable to what other developed nations provide? Put another way: has our government at least the potential economic resources to support its citizens sufficiently to prevent the dangers inherent in a seriously unsatisfied citizenry?

For the amount of money produced by the U.S. economy, we can look at the Federal Reserve Board's periodic *Z-1 Flow of Funds Statement*. In this report, Federal Reserve economists tabulate total monetary equity registered within the U.S., broken down into two categories: financial and non-financial assets. Financial assets are defined as currency and securities at market value, while non-financial assets include tangible assets, not easily converted into money.

In 2011 it reported total financial assets in the U.S. at $156.86 trillion, of which private accounts held 93.12 percent and U.S. federal, state, and local governments together held 6.68 percent.

I focus here on financial assets, money available for profitable investment or purchase of goods and services. That $156.86 trillion of American financial assets in 2011 amounted to half a million dollars for every man, woman, and child of the 2011 U.S. census.

Of particular interest was a further breakdown of private wealth held by categories of the population. In this breakdown, the most affluent 10 percent of households possessed 69.29 percent of total U.S. wealth of which about $45 trillion could be estimated as financial assets. This was an underestimate. It did not include financial and other valuable assets held abroad, undisclosed, in banks, tax shelters, and art warehouses by wealthy Americans and businesses. These undisclosed assets are variously estimated somewhere in the trillions of dollars.

The sheer magnitude of the approximately $45 trillion of reported financial assets held by that top ten percent is hard to comprehend. To give a workforce perspective, just *one* trillion of those $45 trillion could hire five million Americans with jobs averaging fifty thousand a year for four years.

In the context of our national debt and its effects on the current economy and job recovery, it seems reasonable to speculate about what redistribution by taxation of just some of the financial assets held by that top percent could have done in the lagging economy and high unemployment of 2011.

Redistribution of 14 of the 45 trillion dollars held by the wealthiest ten percent would have wiped out the 2011 national debt and thereby given a huge stimulus to the economy.

That sacrifice of the top ten percent would have caused little or no impairment to their life styles but would have removed the motivation of the political right to enforce government austerity with its inhibitory effect on public service jobs and economic recovery.

Paying off the debt would have removed much business uncertainty about the immediate future of the economy as well as the all-consuming political maneuvering over the national debt in Congress. A reenergized economy with increased consumer confidence and spending would have provided real incentives for private business investment and thereby given a boost to economic expansion and job creation.

Using those 2011 Federal Reserve figures, a transfer of $14 trillion of just the financial assets of the top 10 percent, would still have left those top households with about the same amount of financial assets as the other 90 percent of Americans as well as about 55 percent of total national wealth.

With their remaining resources, the top ten percent would still have had most of U.S. industrial capacity in their possession or control and retained unequaled election and lobbying power in current U.S politics. Profits from their business interests would have increased in any resulting economic expansion. With economic vitality increasing, jobs and revenues on the increase, and debt obligations removed, federal revenues would have increased and some of it become available for nation-enhancing initiatives: resumption of public investments in national infrastructure, education, and basic research.

Republican arguments against such an asset redistribution hinge on the capital those top households have for potential business investment: reduce their investment capital and you also reduce business investment and creation of jobs. This argument side-steps the obvious. They still would have a great deal of discretionary capital to invest. And with more of America's financial assets and discretionary income in more hands down the affluence ladder, there still would be investments of discretionary capital in U.S. stocks and bonds but in smaller increments and by more people.

American banks and public agencies like the *Small Business Administration* would still have plenty of money to loan for promising business investment. But the real difficulty with the Republican argument is that there doesn't seem to be any historical evidence that higher taxes on top incomes and less accumulation of assets at the top inhibit job creation and GDP growth.

For example, the Census Bureau compiled a massive study, the *Longitudinal Business Database,* that tracked 23 million businesses and number of jobs from 1977 to 2009. Examination of those data show that the *rate* of job creation trended downward during this period, starting at an annual rate of around 7.5 in 1977 and declining with variations to a rate of around 4.2 by 2009. This decline was not stopped or reversed when taxes on the wealthy were reduced by Republican administrations in the 1980's. Cutting taxes on high incomes by half in the 1980's did, however, accelerate the accumulation of wealth for the upper few percent of households. After those tax cuts, the historical data show that accumulation of wealth at the top accelerated while the rate of job creation trended downward.

These data are consistent with a view that the more private capital diverted into financial speculation, the more the rate of business investment and job creation is reduced in goods and services. The historical record does not refute Republican claims that wealthy investors put money into business growth and innovation. They do. The data, however, are consistent with a view that business and job-promoting investments are only a small fraction of their investments; that most of their investments have more to do with wealth enhancement or conservation than with business innovation and new job creation. Strong and sustained GDP growth between 1950 and 1970 occurred when taxes on top incomes were 70% and 25 – 27% for capital gains. Those rates were much higher than today and accumulation of wealth at the top was much slower while businesses and the economy did very well under those tax burdens.

Queried whether lowering taxes would produce economic expansion, a bipartisan *Congressional Research Service* study

found that lowering the income tax on top incomes did not significantly increase savings, business investments, or productivity.
Another study lasting over sixty years by the Syracuse University
economist Leonard Burman found *no* relationship between variations in capital gains taxes and economic growth. These findings are confirmed in Graph 5.

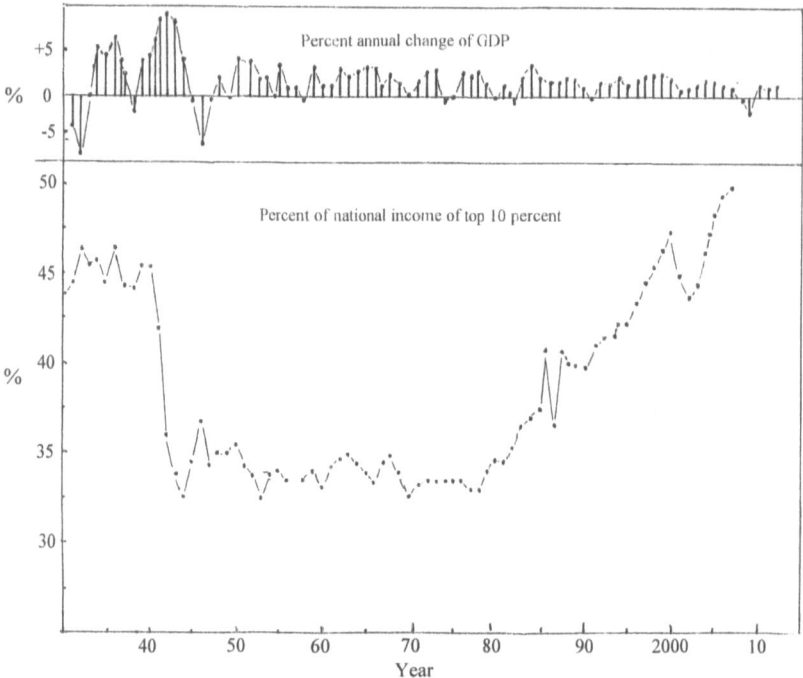

Graph 5   Annual percent of GDP change (length of upper bars) in
relation to the percent of national income held by the top ten percent
of earners in the U.S.(lower line). Data from Piketty and Saez, 2006
update. (The top 10 percent represents families making $104,700
or more annually).

If increasing accumulation of wealth in top households cor-
relates with GDP expansion, there is no sign of it in this historical
graph. Note that as the top-earning households increase their

percent of national wealth after the 1980's, the amount of GDP growth tends downward.

This relationship at the least argues that increasing accumulation of wealth in top households does *not* correlate with GDP growth or job creation. The fact that GDP growth consistently tends downward as inequality of income and wealth increases more probably is telling us that very wealthy households find it safer to commit most of their discretionary income to safe, diverse financial investment than to the work, uncertainty, and higher taxes of investment in goods and service businesses.

If we look at the poor employment record of the economy from 2009 – 2015 and the vast amount of U.S. financial assets held by that upper few percent of households, another important question emerges. Is it in the interest of the nation, its economy, or its business community for such enormous amounts of capital to remain in private ownership and unavailable for business investment and consumer spending?

The Republican claim that business investments by the wealthy are essential for economic expansion and job creation is so prominent in Republican rhetoric but supported by so few facts that Republican leaders need to explain their reasons to the American people why the super wealthy should be allowed, through current tax policies, to retain and keep increasing such a high proportion of American financial assets. This question is far too important to ignore.

In 2015, while corporate profits and the stock markets grew robustly, millions U.S. workers were still out of work seven years after the Great Recession of 2008. For those millions of unemployed who are losing homes, using up retirement savings, and facing an insecure old age, the current situation is an embarrassment for a nation with an economy and private holdings of wealth as great as ours.

In considering possible tax strategies, the American people and their government both need to confront the fact that a significant part of deficit spending has been due to involvement in foreign conflicts for which there has been *no enabling taxation*. Rather than making unpopular taxing decisions necessary for funding such authorized expenditures, Congresses have paid for foreign wars and natural catastrophes the easy way: using ad hoc appropriations. They are simply kicking the unpopular tax support can down the road, and putting the cost onto the tab at the public store for future politicians and Americans.

Financial resources of the United States are enormous but finite. There are never enough to satisfy the needs of all. Especially in an economic slump, existing financial resources are needed for job-supported consumption in the domestic goods and services economy. It is this consumption that *allows* business investment and job creation. In the third quarter of 2012, the financial sector of the U.S. economy, with less than seven percent of U.S. workers, was acquiring over 30 percent of U.S. corporate profits. Such outsized profits in financial sectors signal the sheer magnitude of U.S. working capital circulating in a vast array of loans, rents, and financial speculations.

In economic recession, both businesses and workers suffer and it is fair to ask whether more of U.S. working capital shouldn't be diverted from financial speculation back into goods and services where productive capacity and most jobs reside.

THE FALTERING AMERICAN DREAM. THE CASE FOR A BETTER FUNDED FEDERAL GOVERNMENT

13

Here, we ask whether our economy is sufficient to support a federal government capable of providing world class amenities for its citizens without damaging the economy. We tackle this question by comparing our taxes, revenues, and government expenditures with those of other developed nations with whom we compete in the global marketplace.

Today, in contrast to the vigorous post-WWII decades of public investment and development, we see signs of trouble. The American dream of potential betterment for most of its citizens is beginning to look unrealistic. At public colleges and universities, state and national funding support have lagged behind rising costs of operation. This has been forcing tuitions up, pricing too many young people out of higher education or leaving nascent careers blighted by high debt. The most recent O.E.C.D. report tells us that Russia now has the highest percent of adults with a university education and the U.S., once first, is now further down the list of nations. Because education and job training (both important but not to be confused) are the very heart of technological advancement and national competitiveness, this trend is seriously troubling.

According to the American Society of Civil Engineers, congestion on our aging highways is costing the nation $101 billion annually in wasted time and fuel while 66,000 of our bridges are in need of repair or replacement. Our rail systems have fallen far behind European and Japanese standards of speed and availability.

Poverty in American has been increasing. The News and Observer newspaper in North Carolina on 2/14/2015 reported that between 1990 and 1999 the median American household income increased 10 percent. Since 2000, however, the median had *decreased* nine percent. The Washington Post (1/16/2015) reported that more than half of all students in U.S. public schools, qualify for public help, being from families whose income qualified them for public assistance.

According to the National Poverty Center at the University of Michigan, the number of Americans living in poverty had increased from 11.1 percent in 1973 to 15.1 percent by 2010. In 2010, over 22 percent of American children under 18 were living in poverty. The Census Bureau reported in 2014 that one in five children were on food stamp assistance. That was sixteen million children, up from nine million in 2007.

In a recent study, the *U.K. Commonwealth Fund* compared eleven large, industrialized nations with respect to the cost and effectiveness of their national health systems. In terms of quality and access to health care, that report ranked the U.K. at the top of the list. The United States was *dead last* of the eleven, even though we spend twice as much per capita for health care as the U.K. Even our national parks are slowly deteriorating from insufficient funding. What in the world is happening? Is the United States becoming too poor to afford public amenities at least comparable to other advanced nations?

In trying to answer this questions, we face an indisputable fact: Since that Great Turning Point in national revenues in the 1980's, our government has been spending more than it receives in revenues through twenty years of conservative administrations and well before the 2007-08 financial crisis and The Affordable Care Act entered the scene. The low tax strategies of conservative administrations have consistently resulted in insufficient tax revenues in the face of steadily increasing costs of government per citizen.

Observing these continuing insufficiencies, it appears that we are becoming a poorer nation. Isn't the wealth created by the American economy sufficient to support American citizens at levels common in other developed nations?

Well, yes. At least in measures of national wealth, we are high on international lists. In 2013, The World Bank listed the U.S. economy as the biggest in the world, worth almost $17 trillion. The International Monetary Fund ranked the U.S. ninth richest in the world in terms of GDP output *per capita*. In 2013, our economy produced $53,101 for every man, woman, and child of the 2013 U.S. census.

And in terms of the wealth of our top earners, the U.S. is far ahead of its competitors. *Forbes Magazine* of March 26, 2012 reported that of the six nations with the most billionaires, the United States was far ahead with 425; Russia, the next highest, had only 96. Joe Nocera of the *New York Times* reported that it took a net worth of $1.1 billion to get on the Forbes-400 list of top wealth that year. And those extraordinary accumulations of personal wealth are not the final word. Those Forbes-400 individuals had *increased* their combined wealth by $200 billion since the preceding year. In terms of our economy, GDP output, and personal wealth of business leaders, we are not poor. Rather, we are at or near the top.

Seeing that we cannot blame the national debt and decline of public services on a national lack of money, we might examine our level of spending on government services compared to other nations. Data in the *CIA Factbook* include government spending *per citizen* for the world's twenty largest, developed nations. In that list, Norway had the highest government expenditure at $40,908 per citizen. The average expenditure of those twenty nations was $16,110. The United States government spent $11,041 per citizen, with only six out of the twenty nations spending less. By this measure, our federal government is not throwing money around. In fact, we are below the average in government dollars spent per citizen in support of government services.

This conclusion also is born out when government spending is expressed as percent of national GDP. The *2014 Index of Economic Freedom*, published by the Heritage Foundation, includes a list of what governments of the world spend. From their world list, I selected eighteen advanced nations, including major European nations plus Australia, Canada, Russia, Israel, China, Brazil, United States, and Japan. The governments of those eighteen nations spent an average of 45.7 percent of their GDP's on governance. The U.S. spent 41.6 percent. Only three out of the eighteen spent less. So, by this criterion too, our spending for government services is well below the average of most other developed nations.

If our government is not overspending by international standards, are we taxing enough? The Heritage Foundation also publishes a list of what nations of the world receive in tax revenues, expressed as percent of their GDP output. Using the same list of eighteen nations, the average tax revenue of those eighteen in 2012 was 35.3 percent of their GDP's. The U.S. tax revenue was 26.9 percent of our GDP, with only one other nation lower on that list! By comparison, we certainly are not overburdening our GDP income with government expenditures. We turn out to be far below the average of competitive nations.

With both the world's largest economy and a large national debt, it might surprise some to see that the U.S. government taxes and spends less of its economic wealth than a large majority of other developed nation. What about our tax base? By international standards, why are we not raising sufficient tax revenue as a percent of our national GDP?

Figures on U.S. tax revenues above were expressed as an aggregate, composed of two major components: individual and corporate taxpayers. A breakdown of these two taxing components is published by the White House *Office of Management and Budget.* Data from these historical tables show a long and steady decrease in the amount of tax revenue collected from U.S. corporations. In 1944 during WWII, corporations contributed 33.9 percent of federal tax revenues while individuals contributed 45.0 percent. By 2012, the corporate share had been reduced to 9.9 percent with individuals contributing 46.2 percent.

This decline in corporate tax contributions can be attributed to many factors. There has been an accumulation of corporate tax loop holes over the years, obtained by lobbying Congress for tax relief due to 'special' circumstances. Corporate tax experts are skillful in utilizing details of international trade agreements and selection of low tax jurisdictions to reduce or eliminate taxes.

The 35 percent federal rate on top corporate incomes is high by international standards but seldom is paid by U.S. companies. What is actually paid is the *effective rate,* the percent of profit actually going to the government. The effective tax rate had been reduced to 12.6 percent of aggregate corporate profits by 2010, a rate little more than a third of the statutory rate. This long decline in corporate tax contributions also is seen in corporate tax revenue as percent of GDP. By this measure, corporate taxes were 6 to 7 percent of GDP just after WWII but had been reduced to between 1 and 2 percent by 2009.

Profits generated in foreign countries and kept in off-shore tax havens, as described in Chapter 2, have sharply curtailed corporate tax contributions to federal revenues. According to analyst Alan Pyke, in early 2014 foreign subsidiaries of American corporations held in overseas tax havens an estimated $2 trillion of profits from foreign investments. An increasingly common stratagem has been to merge with a foreign company in a country with lower corporate taxes, using that country as the company's tax base.

Another tax-evading practice, involves the 'performance' bonuses paid to corporate executives. As described earlier, total compensations paid to top U.S. corporate executives are generally higher than those paid in other developed nations. That difference is primarily due to bonuses paid in dollars, stock, or stock options. Those bonuses, treated under current law as operating expenses, amount to many millions of dollars in big companies. As such, they can be subtracted from the company's taxable income. The *Institute for Policy Studies and Campaign for America's Future* examined a sample of 90 publically owned corporations. They found that those companies, by treating executive bonus packages as operational expense, reduced taxes between 953 million and $1.6 billion in the three years 2009 - 2011.

One would think that bonus money paid to top executives and off the company's books would then be subject to tax on the executive's income at a high tax bracket. Yes, but only partially. Wealthy people reduce taxes on personal income through trusts, charities, and tax-free investments. Commonly, these huge bonuses are invested in financial speculations where dividends, interest, and capital gains are taxed at the lower rates charged on unearned income.

Thus, the billions of dollars of performance bonuses paid to U.S. corporate executives result not only in lowered tax revenue but a substantial redistribution of money earned by work in goods and service sectors into lower-taxed financial speculations. How much U.S. working capital are we talking about here?

Federal Reserve economists keep track of American financial assets, defined as currency and securities at market value. In 2013 they reported that 70.7 percent of America's total wealth was in financial assets while 29.3 percent was in tangible assets. And this share of America's financial wealth had grown more than three percent in four years.

In these reports, we see a steady transfer of more and more U.S. productive capital, earned in goods and services, into financial sectors. This transfer is motivated by lower taxes on financial income and exacerbated by the low tax policies on high earned incomes favored by Republican administrations. Those low tax policies give wealthy individuals and financial institutions more to invest in financial sectors.

There is a slightly different understanding of these movements of financial capital when you remember that financial assets represent not only money invested for making money in goods and services, but also money available for buying those goods and services. Business investments in the most attractive goods and services are of no avail if there is no money out there to buy them. Working capital is needed for *both* trickle-down business investment and trickle-up purchasing power. Trickle down investment is *enabled* and largely controlled by the amount of U.S. financial assets available for trickle up consumption.

As described in Chapter 11, most of America's working capital ends up in possession of the top few percent of America's earners. Is this out of line with other developed countries? Some 2013 numbers were available on the *mybudget360* website. There, we see, in the U.S. and seven other major developed nations, how much of their national wealth has been accumulated by the top ten percent of earners. The wealthiest top ten percent of the earners in those eight countries held an average of 49.6 percent of their national wealth. The top ten percent in the U.S. had 74 percent!

Unfortunately for the bottom 90 percent of Americans, and for our economy as a whole, we are far ahead of the rest of the developed world in the unequal distribution of national wealth, especially of America's financial assets, the circulating life-blood of the economy.

On the basis of information presented here, it is apparent that we could increase tax revenues without compromising our economy any more than our international competitors. Given the unusually high inequality in the possession of America's working capital, the best places to increase tax revenue in a tax policy overhaul would be from corporations and our top earners whose compensations, wealth, and unearned profits are a greater proportion of national wealth and income than those of other nations.

BIG MONEY IN AMERICAN POLITICAL ELECTIONS

14

We now look at the corruption of America's political system through the need for campaign money and describe how that corruption was amplified by the Supreme Court Citizens United decision in 2010.

"Great corporations exist only because they are created and safeguarded by our institutions; and it is therefore our right and our duty to see that they work in harmony with these institutions." Theodore Roosevelt (1901)

"... ... all contributions by corporations to any political committee or for any political purpose should be forbidden by law." Theodore Roosevelt (1905)

Most of us know our constitution establishes an *equal influence* for all citizens in the election of a government official: one vote for each citizen, whether rich or poor, white or colored. It also guarantees the right of all citizens to express their opinions in public about candidates for government positions. But the right of equal influence on election outcomes becomes corrupted when a wealthy citizen gains unequal influence by the use of money to magnify his/her opinions beyond what a poorer citizen can afford.

A major and well-recognized division of economic interests exists in our political world: business vs labor. The necessary interaction of the two interests is obvious because each supplies what the other cannot, and each needs the other for their economic survival. Despite being functionally joined at the hip, there is tension between them for a share of the economic pie that their interaction provides. This tension is expressed by political contention in the Congress over laws and regulations that ultimately determine what share of the economic pie each will get. It is a dramatic change in that traditional political struggle that we look at in this chapter.

The political campaigns of 2012 were overwhelmed by a deluge of super political action committee (PAC) money. The sheer magnitude of this *non-campaign* money is a powerful indicator of how influential money has become in American politics. The difference in political spending between business and labor interests is also an indicator of increasing inequality of money and political influence between the two.

First, let's get some idea of the scale of money spent in the 2012 elections. The total spending by both presidential campaigns, according to a New York Times report shortly after the elections, was a record-breaking $2.253 billion. If expenditures on congressional campaigns are included the total was $6.3 billion!

This massive expenditure has other disturbing elements besides amount. The new rules generated by the Supreme Court's 2010 *Citizens United* decision and exacerbated by their more recent *McCutcheon vs FEC* decision, have left in place restrictions on money given to political campaigns but have given the green light to non-campaign advertising money as constitutionally-protected free speech – even to organizations like corporations, labor unions, and super PACs. Those decisions have opened wide the flood gates of non-campaign money to influence election results.

Individuals, through special- interest PAC'S, are now allowed unlimited spending for electioneering ads. Because of these changes in law, there are now two kinds of money in campaigns: money raised under legal limits and spent by the campaigns and money raised and spent by non-campaign individuals or organizations with no legal limits.

For Democrats, their supportive PAC's spent $66.5 million, or 7 percent of what the Obama campaign legally raised and spent. On the Republican side, the supportive PAC's spent $398.4 million, or 46 percent of what the Romney campaign raised and spent. Of the five super PAC's with the greatest resources, $92.4 million was spent against Romney and $257.6 million against Obama.

These figures illustrate a large imbalance of private money support between the two parties and their candidates. Later figures on the election by US PIRG (an independent consumer organization) found that of super PAC donations, $505 million was raised from only 159 wealthy donors. Of that amount, the political network organized and heavily subsidized by the wealthy Koch brothers, provided more than $400 million for Republican candidates. The Koch organization contributions amounted to about twice the amount invested by the top ten labor unions combined. In this case, the two Koch brothers bought more advertising influence than tens or hundreds of thousands of voting union members. This disparity emphasizes what most of us already know: it is through super PAC's that people of wealth are able to step around the legal limit of campaign donations and buy extraordinary *influence* in determining the result of elections.

Two unpleasant aspects of the big-spending PAC's were borne by the public. Contributors to many of those super PAC's did not need to disclose their identities and accept responsibility for what was broadcast. As a consequence, most ads sponsored by them filled the airways with negative character or behavior attributions about opposing candidates rather than their positions on the issues that are important to Americans in general.

The other unpleasant aspect involved solicitations for contributions. The extensive use of electronic media to ask for donations was irritating to millions of households in both constancy and intensity. In this horse race for campaign money, an observer from Mars easily could have concluded that political offices were auctioned off to candidates who raised the most money.

There is a long history of efforts to eliminate this corrupting influence of money in the political process. The idea from the first was to make elections dependent on what the candidates stood for, not by how much money they had for campaign propaganda.

The first such law was enacted in 1867. It prohibited men with federal positions from soliciting campaign contributions from their employees. Since then, legislation has been introduced repeatedly to remove the corruption of the election process by money. Almost all effective attempts have been defeated. Successful opposition, of course, comes from relatively wealthy voters whose power derives from the need of candidates for their contributions of money to win election to office.

The *Tillman Act* of 1907, among other examples, forbade corporations and banks from making direct contributions to candidates. The *Federal Corrupt Practices Act* of 1925 limited the amount of money that could be contributed to political candidates by individuals.

In 1964 the addition of the 24th amendment to the constitution spoke to a closely related aspect of money in political contests. Poll taxes in many states had been enacted to discourage or prevent poorer voters from voting. The amendment ruled that possession or use of money cannot be a requirement for voting because such requirements put poorer citizens at a disadvantage at the voting poles. This was a constitutional protection of voting rights for less affluent citizens, keeping the necessity for money out of access to the voting booth.

In 2002 Congress finally passed a more effective election law aimed at getting most money out of federal elections. The Bipartisan *Campaign Reform Act* (McCain – Feingold) prohibited individuals, unions, or corporations from making 'electioneering communications' mentioning a federal political candidate by name during periods of time crucially important in election campaigns: 30 days before a primary or 60 days before a general election. This was a huge step forward and consistent with previous laws aimed at keeping the use of non-campaign, special interest money out of campaigns.

Then, in 2010 the Supreme Court dropped its bomb. It affirmed an appeal from the Citizens United Corporation: an appeal denied by lower courts on the basis of existing anticorruption campaign laws. In a 5 to 4 decision, the Justices ruled that corporations and labor unions could not be prohibited from spending *unlimited* amounts of money in *in*direct support of political parties or candidates because such denial would violate their First Amendment right of free speech. In part, Justice Kennedy wrote for the majority: " ...If the First Amendment has any force, it prohibits Congress from fining or jailing citizens, or associations of citizens, from simply engaging in political speech." One can wonder if that should have been ... from simply investing in televised propaganda.

This decision seemed to define money offered in support of a candidate to be corrupt only *when* the money is offered. If money is offered to an already-elected office holder to gain the donor's wishes, the Justices recognized it as corruption. If the same money is used to enable a candidate to gain a political office capable of granting the donor's wishes, the Justices viewed that as a free speech right.

The difficulty with this distinction is that if a candidate, aided by a donor's money, is elected to office, the new office-holder will find the smiling donor at his/her door, reminding the new office-holder of the gift. We can safely assume that the larger the donor's campaign gift, the more gratitude and obligation the new office-holder will experience in responding to that smile.

This sense of obligation is especially acute since the office holder, as soon as elected will have to start soliciting campaign funds for the next election. If someone argues that the campaign donor made the gift, not as a means of getting the official the power to grant the donor's request but only as the free speech right to state a political opinion, that person should wonder why so many individuals and organizations are willing to spend millions to simply articulate their opinions.

The answer, of course, is that someone with much money can afford the risk, and the political rewards obviously must be worth the risk. But, by whatever name you use, the act of giving money beyond legal limits for immediate or future legislative favor is political corruption: the use of money to enhance or ensure the probability of government action favorable to the donor's interests.

In a practical sense, the First Amendment free speech guarantee is commonly interpreted to mean that citizens may voice opinions in public without fear of reprisal by authority. On its face, the court's decision was an affirmation of the right of people to express unpopular or even anti-government opinions in public without fear of authoritarian punishment.

But a another crucial difficulty with the Supreme Court's *Citizens United* decision arises because today the right to freely express opinion on government actions has almost no *influence* at all unless broadcast to a wide public audience, most effectively before elections. Broadcasting to a wide political audience requires money – lots of it. People of wealth and their political action committees have a money advantage for achieving their political ambitions by being able to buy expensive national TV time.

The high court decision has had the unfortunate consequence of allowing non-campaign investments to have great, often decisive, *influence* on an election outcome. In so doing, it also has contributed to an embarrassing degradation of the quality of political 'speech' (e.g. personal disparagement; questionable fact; quotations out of context; almost complete absence of substantive candidate position on issues).

A money advantage is most easily recognized in local elections where political advertising is accomplished by street and yard signs that endlessly reiterate a candidate's name. Issues and political positions or experience are not mentioned on the signs. Just familiarizing voters with a candidate's name is what counts in a voting booth. Such advertising has everything to do with familiarity of a name and nothing to do with 'free speech' about the qualifications of a candidate.

In a political contest, a candidate who could afford a thousand signs and her opponent who could afford only one hundred both have the protected right to put out their signs. The difference in the number of signs, however, has everything to do with the amount of money spent and the probability of election success.

The high court's decision has had the unfortunate consequence of giving contributions of money in a political contest as much, or probably more, influence on the election outcome than candidates' qualifications and opinions as expressed in their campaigns. Only this can explain the eagerness of partisan supporters of both parties to contribute such exorbitant amounts of money.

Every voter who goes to the poles does so with many concerns: jobs, wages, health, environment, safe cities, etc. Their vote represents a balance of their concerns. Corporations, on the other hand, have a single goal: maximization of return on investment. It is a goal which gives high priority to reduction of labor costs. This priority motivates them to invest in cheaper foreign labor, labor-saving mechanization, and the lowest wage the labor market will allow. The goal directly confounds the national need for *more* and better-paid American jobs to support trickle-up consumption in the economy.

A corporate leader legally can use *company* money to lobby Congress. This is a powerful tool in achieving legislative goals for his/her company, a tool that most citizens cannot afford. Why should company executives be given the additional power of using *company* money to influence an election?

For corporations that have sold ownership shares to the public, can profits due stock-holder owners be diverted to political ends over which they, as voters have no say? It seems to me that giving this privilege to corporate executives, the Supreme Court has departed from the constitution's intent of one vote (influence on an elections' outcome) for each citizen.

The distribution of financial assets has become very unequal in America with a lion's share in possession of the owners and managers of big businesses, many of which are now realizing much profit from their foreign subsidiaries as well as from American consumers. More U.S. corporate attention now focuses on foreign politics and markets. Their dominant possession of money translates directly into the political power to control legislation in their favor. And corporate power has become ever greater as the contravening power of labor unions is progressively weakened by utilization of foreign labor, replacement of labor by mechanization, and active business and political suppression of labor unions.

"The misfortune of a republic ... happens when the people are gained (*taken advantage of*) by bribery and corruption: in this case they (*the people*) grow indifferent to public affairs and avarice becomes their predominate passion." Baron de Montesquieu, an Enlightenment philosopher

A BETTER WAY TO ELECT POLITICIANS TO PUBLIC OFFICE

15

Pay to play. This sums up pretty well how political campaigns are currently funded and legislative outcomes influenced by contributions of money. There are much better ways to run and fund elections. Here, I outlne two that would be more in tune with the constitutional goal of giving all citizens equal influence in the election of their representatives to the federal government.

In the preceding chapter I highlighted the amounts and unequal distribution of special interest money going into the election of federal politicians. We also know that elected officials are open to expensive lobbying. Both practices have in common the requirement for money. Both political parties felt these election needs in the 2012 campaigns and legally raised unprecedented amounts. The expenditures occurred at a time when the federal government, to which all federal candidates aspired, was deeply in debt and unable to fund many of its services at optimal levels.

The fatal flaw in the system, of course, is the dependence on voluntary contributions of money to get elected in the first place. But after a successful election campaign, the donors who funded the successful campaign have first claim on the official's time and influence: The greater the donation, the greater the chance of favorable attention.

But even after a successful campaign, the need for money to fund the next election campaign again becomes a high priority in the congressional day calendar. It has been estimated that members of Congress spend 30-70 percent of their time raising money for their next campaign. Pay to play. Unfortunately, that describes the current need for, and influence of, money: putting money into the hand of an office-holder for special consideration.

There is public recognition of this as a major flaw. The Pew Research Center found in 2010 that 68 percent of respondents disapproved of the *Citizens United* decision, including 65 percent of Republican voters. In 1964 29 percent of voters believed that government was run by big money-oriented interests looking out for themselves. In 2013 almost three times that many agreed!

Many efforts over the years, sometimes bipartisan, to eradicate the intrusion of money into political elections have been initiated in Congress by courageous legislators. These efforts always have been fiercely opposed by money-accumulating interests. Unfortunately, the influence of money has been so ingrained in our elections for so long and is so heavily protected in Congress that we roll our eyes heavenward and shrug our shoulders. Is there *any* solution that can address this increasingly serious flaw in our election system?

In 2002 the *Bipartisan Campaign Reform Act* (McCain – Feingold) was passed. It was a major step. It controlled the amount of money given to campaigns by individuals and organizations, and forbad "electioneering communications" by non-campaign entities for 30 days before a primary election and 60 days before a general one. This had the effect of eliminating the influence of richer donors, capable of buying TV time, at least during the pre-election campaigning months.

The elimination of non-campaign electioneering communications during these periods was both insightful and important: it was recognition that those months of pre-election campaigning are unusually important for Americans when the candidates and their campaigns inform voters who they are and what they stand for. Prohibiting non-campaign electioneering during these times forbad propagandistic ads which are vulnerable to factual distortion and psychological manipulation.

A practical modification of the McCain-Feingold legislation could prohibit the current outsider propaganda during those important campaign months without eliminating the *equal* free speech right of everyone to air their campaign opinions. Such a modification would only require that electioneering expressions be submitted to the campaign of their choice during the critical pre-election months. It would then be a candidate or campaign manager looking for telling political arguments, not a TV executive looking for revenue, that made a decision about whether, or how, to air a submission.

Such a modification would allow a chance for free expression of opinions from *everyone* during those pre-election periods. It would ensure that opinions heard during the pre-election campaigns were not broadcast because of a requirement for money. Candidates' campaigns could air any submission deemed helpful to their campaign, using legally controlled campaign money and taking responsibility for the truth and relevance of it.

Such a modification would ensure the right of everyone to submit their ideas and opinions to public media. The only requirement would be that any kind of public airing of an electioneering communication could not be purchased. It would allow televised interviews, op-ed pieces in news media, or submissions purchased for publication by a magazine editor on the basis of quality and relevance to the publication's readership. The expression of political opinion would thus be available equally to all citizens.

An interesting agreement by political contestants that largely eliminated outside money and ads emerged in the 2012 Senate campaign in Massachusetts. Although it did not have the permanence of legislative law, it proved to be remarkably effective when endorsed and honored by both contenders. Senate candidates Elizabeth Warren and Scott Brown agreed to sign a "People's Pledge."

Both candidates told supporters to keep their money and ads out of their campaigns. If an outside group purchased an ad, the campaign receiving the benefit would have to make an offsetting donation to a charity of the opponent's choice. It worked. Almost all outside money was kept out of that contest. This idea has much to offer and hopefully its beneficial intent will influence future elections and, may we hope, legislative action.

For a solution that would take all of the power of special interest money out of our federal elections, public funding comes immediately to mind. It would remove most of the power of moneyed interests to buy legislative favor. In addition, if limits also were imposed on how quickly a retiring lawmaker could be given a lucrative consulting job with an applicant's company, this corruptive power also would be eliminated.

Once elected through a publically-funded campaign, successful candidates would be able to spend *all of their* time studying legislative issues, consulting experts, examining the experiences of others, and preparing to create or support legislation according to their informed judgment and what their voting base felt was in their interest. No longer would it be necessary to spend valuable time pandering to the interests of donors rather than the needs of constituents and the nation.

This clear and universal understanding about removing the corruption of money in national elections has driven past attempts to legislate public funding and helped create the present publically-funded option available to political candidates. The first viable version of the current public funding law was passed in 1971 and amended in subsequent acts in 1974, 76, 79, 84, and 1993. It is currently available to candidates for federal offices with limits on how much can be obtained from the U.S. treasury. It is funded by a voluntary check-off box on personal income tax returns, amounting to $3 per checked off return. To be effective today because of the Supreme Court's Citizens United decision, such a public law would now need legislation to prevent non-campaign donations of media time or money during the pre-election primary and general elections months.

The public funding law has been used in past elections. Unfortunately, it is now useless because there are *no limits on how much can be donated by supporters* if the public option is rejected. Therefore, no candidate could afford to accept public funding and allow an opponent to receive more money from outsiders. Expensive media time is still central in the election efforts of a candidate.

A positive correlation between money spent by super PACs in the 2014 midterm elections and the success of the candidate has been confirmed by statistical analyses. Such corruption is readily recognized by those not completely blinded by party bias. The corruptive influence of money is also confirmed by the sheer magnitude of money offered to help candidates.

If the presidential candidates of the 2012 election had opted to take advantage of existing public funding, each would have been given $91.2 million. This is about one-twelfth of the record-breaking amounts their campaigns actually raised and spent. But the amount still would have offered a fair opportunity for a candidate to make a substantive case for election because the opposing candidates would have the same amount.

In terms of the campaigns themselves, how much would taxpayers have had to pay on their 2011 IRS returns to fund the record-breaking expenditures of both presidential campaigns of 2012?

In 2012, the two presidential campaigns' expenditures amounted to 0.077 percent of federal tax revenues of 2011. Using a yearly income tax to fund a presidential election every fourth year would have required a *yearly* tax of $3.85 on an income of $20,000; $9.62 on $50,000; $19.25 on $100,000; $192.50 on $1,000,000.

The 0.077 percent tax on corporate profits and union dues also would be fair since the Supreme Court's misguided Citizens United decision giving corporations and unions the status of voting citizens. It seems probable that funding at half the 2012 campaign amounts would still allow candidates to present themselves and their and position on issues thoroughly and fairly since both sides would have no advantage in advertising money.

Because all outside electioneering communication through public media would need to be prohibited, the corrupting influence of money and a wealth advantage would no longer be in play. Under a public funding law, every citizen would still have equal *free speech rights* to submit their opinions to a campaign for public airing or to news media as long as the submission was not a purchased access. A public funding law also would have to prohibit acceptance of lucrative job offers or other perks from companies, unions, or political parties for at least two years after leaving public office.

The small 0.077% income tax for public support of federal campaigns should be welcomed by active, wealthy taxpayers because it would mean a much smaller contribution for election results than what they risked in 2012 for a particular party or candidate. Those at the lower end of the income spectrum for which four dollars a year might be significant or for those with insufficient interest to care about the election, the small tax would procure a considerable benefit: much fewer of their TV and radio hours polluted with political blather.

History has shown that fierce opposition will arise against any law mandating publically-funded elections. The opposition, of course, will come from those with the means to purchase influence. The expected arguments have always been "Why fix it if it isn't broken? Why shouldn't a successful person have the right to donate more than some unsuccessful bum? Why shouldn't anyone who could afford it have the free speech right to buy TV time or newspaper space?"

Such arguments, of course, are irrelevant in speaking to the issue of *equal opportunity* for free political speech *for all* citizens, at least during the special times of electioneering campaigns. During these nationally important campaigns, public funding would be the most powerful way of preserving the free speech rights intention of the constitution while eliminating the corrupting influence of money.

In my opinion, we must not let wide-spread political cynicism, which is palpably increasing in America, get in the way of public determination to restore a more broadly representative governance through public funding of elections. Such cynicism just shrugs it shoulders and hopelessly complains about the way things are going — so why try?

We cannot be overcome by such stoical or cynical feelings and survive as a nation in today's global world.

SUMMING UP

16

It is easy to find fault in the operations of a gigantic institution like the U.S. government, designed by our founders to be responsive to the collective needs of all voting citizens. The challenge in today's changing world is to find ways of safe-guarding that egalitarian vision so that government sensitivity to multitudinous needs is retained in practice and not captured by a rich and powerful few. Here are some ruminations about major problems we face in trying to realize the American dream for the betterment of our nation and all of our children.

B y far, the most fundamental and gravest problem that dis-torts the egalitarian hopes of our founders for the common dreams of *all* of our citizens is the overwhelming influence of money in the election of Congress and the President.

Currently, it is money that dominates pay-to-play politics, enables and protects high inequality of wealth and power, and exacerbates party intransigence in Congress. Much of that party intransigence derives from the political need for well-heeled or multitudinous supporters to fund the next campaign. Those mon-ey-requiring pressures distract politicians from the multitudinous needs of their constituents, requiring the use of much of their valuable legislative time to pander for the money to win their next election. This distraction exists at all levels of government but is most dangerous to our egalitarian ideals at the federal level.

The most urgently-needed solution to this monetary corruption is reestablished governmental sensitivity to the full range of voter interests. Such sensitivity was intended by our founders with their constitutionally mandated one-citizen-one-vote election process. It was meant to give a small but *equal* chance for every citizen to influence the make-up of their government and its actions. Decisive influence would be attained by the number of votes cast not the amount of money obtained for the advertising campaign.

The most direct and cost-effective way to curb the current power and influence of money in our political decision-making is to mandate publically-funded elections. I have demonstrated in Chapter 15 how this could be accomplished, ensuring that everyone, rich or poor, has the same chance of influencing other voters with his or her free speech and obtaining their preferred outcome.

Public funding of federal elections would restore our founders' intention of equal influence for every voter. But to preserve that change against political majorities in Congress, it will need an amendment to our constitution. But only wide public appreciation of the current situation, brought on by national debate with wide coverage, could get the ball rolling for a such a national referendum. It would galvanize the necessary public attention if one of the political parties or a presidential candidate put the issue front and center during an election campaign — or raised the issue in the early years of a presidential term of office.

In a national debate on the issue, defenders of current money-dominated electioneering would have to identify themselves and justify retaining the system. A national debate should be welcomed by both parties on considerations of fairness, constitutional intent, and costs.

A particularly sorry manipulation of elections is the

gerrymandering of election districts in the states. This blatant manipulation of voting districts guarantees election success for one party, rendering elections in those districts non-competitive and useless. This is clearly a degradation of the electoral system, publically acknowledged by both parties.

As of this writing, several forward-looking states have corrected this electioneering abomination: Iowa, Washington, Arizona, and Idaho with others in various exploratory stages. The new laws put responsibility for drawing district borders in the hands of non-partisan commissions.

Legislative intransigence in Washington has been exacerbated by centralized party control. This control is most egregiously manifested in Grover Norquist's and the far political right's power to extract a pledge from Republican candidates that they will *never* vote for a tax increase.

Such a maneuver eliminates the primary responsibility of legislators: to respond to demonstrated public needs and their funding requirements. Disobedience to such a pledge can result in loss of party support and even a well-funded primary challenge from a same-party contender. Although party pressure is practiced by both parties in promoting voting unity in Congress, it is especially dangerous today for a Republican congressman or senator to vote for something central party bosses did not approve.

Much of the current party rancor seems to stem from intransigent central party ideology, which by its nature is distanced from grass roots concerns. An obvious manifestation of this centralized influence is the *American Legislative Exchange Council* (ALEC), a central body which advocates and even crafts potential legislation for Republican legislators at state and federal levels. This kind of action, especially when backed by threats of loss of campaign money or well-funded competition in primary campaigns, seems too much concerned with a national agenda for attracting serious campaign money. ALEC is an organization funded prominently by wealthy contributors for their business-oriented political interests. It acts to define their particular political needs. Its position of well-heeled authority makes it politically dangerous for a Republican politician to press too hard for a personal position or a local concern of constituents that did not conform to ALEC's party position.

We should watch with interest the California experiment of pitting against each other in general elections the two primary candidates who have the most votes, *regardless of party*. Instead of nominees confined by party mandates, the general election involves the two candidates who receive the most votes from all voters of the contested jurisdiction. Such a system may help to reduce a candidate's subservience to, and fear of, central party control, promoting more campaign attention to the needs of voters in their particular jurisdiction.

A major concern in this book has been the *per citizen* cost of government services: costs growing faster than inflation and population. Large increases are traceable to many of the federal departments and agencies. Over the years, proposed budgets have been scrutinized, adjusted, and approved by administrations and congressional majorities of both parties.

Both budgetary and unbudgeted demands too often have been inadequately supported by taxes, especially after the Great Turning Point that marked the introduction of lower taxes as a means of reducing government while stimulating economic growth. Those lowered tax laws, coupled with increasing spending, have continually increased the national debt and caused serious insufficiencies in congressionally approved government services.

Among the federal agencies, healthcare and combined defense and homeland security have, by far, the biggest budgets. Defense and health needs are relatively easy to understand. Defense budgets involve continuous modernization of equipment and training that is needed to counter threats at home, on borders, and abroad. Maintenance of good health is becoming more technically complex with increasingly costly drugs, medical services, and surgical interventions entering the system. We must determine through time and experience how costs in the current law can be contained. One thing is certain: the nation's economy cannot afford to treat everybody at all stages of life with all that medical technology can provide. I am confident though, that like the evolution of the automobile, the health care law too will eventually evolve into an efficient, cost-effective system.

Other recently revealed inadequacies in government services are showing up in the Internal Revenue Service, Veterans Affairs, and Bureau of Land Management. Unusually rapid increases in the budgets of Justice and Environmental Protection also give us warning of increasing pressures on these vital federal responsibilities.

For discovering and correcting unnecessary or duplicate federal services, we must pay more public attention to the operations of the non-partisan Inspectors General. These important officials are assigned to every major federal agency. The current 73 Inspectors General have authority and a mandate to detect and call the attention of executive and legislative leaders to redundancies, irregular or illegal procedures, theft, and inefficiency in their assigned agency.

In my opinion, their work and reports should be more widely and routinely recognized in the media to enhance public awareness of their actions and findings. That might reduce the politically-motivated braying and hollering from the out-of-power party about how inefficient (dumb, corrupt, lying . .) the in-power party is. These constantly articulated negative assertions decrease the confidence in, and increase the cynicism of, Americans about their only government.

Because of the high level of income and wealth inequality that now exists, legislators should now pay more attention to the distribution of America's financial assets. Too many of those assets, accumulated by top households, have become unavailable for the necessary services that government renders for the good of American businesses and the citizens who support them. Those necessary services include public programs in education, professional training, basic research, and public infrastructure. The jobs in these services and the public value they produce are integral to the economy and essential to American businesses and their ability to invest for growth.

Far too many assets are being diverted into financial speculations that aid wealth accumulation for individuals and businesses but are of little or no advantage to the economy. There is no positive correlation between the percent of American capital that households have for business investment and the growth rate of the American economy or increase in its jobs.

A question emerges: If a more substantial portion of U.S. financial assets were available to the government, wouldn't that money, if invested in jobs in public infrastructure, education, and basic research provide more consumers and value to the American economy than if left circulating in financial speculations for private wealth enhancement?

The accumulation of private wealth through talent and enterprise is both good for the country and inevitable. The argument here is one only of quantity. There seems to be a general assumption that the supply of working capital in the U.S. is unlimited: Who cares how much wealthy people accumulate as long as their success doesn't impact my livelihood? If such an assumption is abroad today, it has little to do with current economic reality.

Substantial gains in national wealth through commercial enterprise have almost all gone to the top few percent of American business and financial executives since the Great Turning Point in taxation policies of the 1980s. Meanwhile, the great majority of Americans have seen their incomes, life styles, and prospects stagnate or diminish. This increasing inequality of income and wealth among Americans directly confounds the American dream of possible betterment for our children. It also is associated with the decline in America's middle class, increasing poverty, and high national debt.

According to the analyses of French economist Thomas Piketty, the top *one* percent of American households hold over thirty percent of American wealth. The bottom fifty percent holds a mere five percent, most of it tied up in homes and long term retirement accounts. Piketty's important contribution is the detailed demonstration that this accumulation of wealth at the top is characteristic of capitalistic economies world-wide and has been occurring for over three hundred years.

This accumulation of working capital in financial sectors is exacerbated by the lower rate of taxation of profits on financial investment than on labor and production. From this historical perspective, the U.S. capitalistic economy thus seems destined to allow the top few percent of business and financial leaders, with more discretionary money, to keep increasing their percent of total national wealth. Is this simply the inevitable trend for free market capitalism?

Such a gloomy projection is not justified by the ups and downs of unequal wealth accumulation in our recent past. The great wars of the 20th century caused major redistributions of top wealth in the U.S. and other capitalistic countries. Wealth for the top few percent decreased as a proportion of national wealth as higher taxes on top wealth became politically possible. Because of World War II: the interests of the money elite and the nation became aligned sufficiently to allow higher taxes on higher incomes.

Without the stress of great wars, however, the political power of wealth has been, and will continue to be, hard to overcome. This is because of the corruption of our election process, a situation that is exploited effectively by more wealthy money-accumulating entrepreneurs.

But a *measured* redistribution of American financial assets, now in personal hands, must be undertaken if the country is not to continually drift toward a too-powerful, money-oriented oligarchy. Allowed to become too great, inequality of wealth and economic opportunity has repeatedly been shown in the history of nations to be violently unstable. In the perspective developed here, to reverse this drift, we can discern a rough outline of what needs to be done to ensure a more equitable distribution of the nation's assets among its citizens.

Unusually high incomes and the accumulations of great wealth are most common in the compensations of top executives of large corporations and financial investment companies and associations. A report in the New York Times of June 8, 2014 recorded the highest CEO compensation of a large corporation in 2013. It was $141,949,280! The *average* CEO compensation of the 200 largest U.S. companies that year was $20,722,490. And that 2013 average was an astounding 32 percent higher than in the previous year!

To moderate this vast movement of assets into financial speculation, a two-tiered tax on profits from financial investment might be considered. For one tier, a low tax on the profits of tightly defined retirement and philanthropic investments in the nation's interest might make sense. For a second tier, an effective tool would be a sharply progressive, single taxation rate on income from *both* earned and unearned sources. This would greatly increase federal revenues and federal debt reduction while eliminating the tax preference for investment in financial speculation.

Robert J. Shiller, a prominent Nobel laureate economist, has suggested a way to calibrate such a policy of progressive taxation to relieve the problem of unequal wealth accumulation. He suggests using the measureable degree of U.S. household income inequality in the calculation of tax levels: the greater the national inequality, the higher the tax on upper incomes — and vice versa. This makes good sense to me as an option for congressional study in a process of tax reform.

Expanded in scope, a similar automatically adjustable tax also could provide a way of meeting the real-world financial needs of government without the political cost. That cost, raising taxes for justifiable reasons, makes elected politicians shy away from tax measures that would actually pay the bills. It would be an improvement over what we popularly term "..kicking the (tax) can down the road" (and accumulating debt). Our political inability to pay the real operational costs of government with the necessary taxes is a structural weakness of out form of government. It is a weakness that urgently needs public discussion and bipartisan consideration for the long term fiscal sustainability of government.

Along with arguments for higher taxation of high wealth, however, it is well to keep reemphasizing that wealth is not a bad thing. Within the limits of national well-being, it is both necessary and desirable. High incomes in general reflect reward for hard work and high talent, a traditional American virtue. Future taxation policies should continue to guarantee the right of outstanding talent to make and keep outstanding compensations and life styles. The donation of money by wealthy individuals through philanthropic legacies, trusts and gifts, have greatly enriched the American culture and nation.

While acknowledging the many benefits to the nation from wealthy individuals, however, some limit on individual wealth needs to be recognized. This is because the amount of financial assets in the nation is not unlimited. As a result, a zero sum calculation begins to apply in which the nation's requirements for maintaining a reasonably satisfied citizenry and a vibrant economy must be given priority over personal wealth accumulation.

Thomas Piketty has suggested a small tax on accumulated wealth. Although impossible to enforce if not supported by other nations, it is an idea to start public discussion on reducing the current, other-worldly levels of private accumulation of financial assets in America.

Corporate tax laws need to be brought up to date. Corporations need to pay a fair tax on their profits, especially since the Supreme Court has now equated their political campaign rights of "free speech" to those of tax-paying citizens.

The current statutory top corporate tax of 35 percent is too high by international standards. The result is that corporate taxation that contributed 27 percent of federal revenues in the 1950's has been reduced by lobbying to a revenue contribution of less than half that by 2013.

In these times of inadequate job opportunities and corporate profits at record highs, corporate leaders need to adequately pay for the services provided by their government: the world's best consumer market for their products, a mantle of world-wide protection for their business activities at home and abroad; a very expensive legal playing field for their transactions; a stable government that enables their consumers' interests and goals. The nation also offers to company employees many amenities for personal growth and the civic and cultural amenities characteristic of a great nation.

There are obvious issues that need to be taken into account in any revision of corporate tax laws. A fair tax on profits made by off-shore corporate subsidiaries must be realized. Tax evasions through tax registration in low-tax state jurisdictions and through exploitation of international trade laws need to be more controlled and brought into line with the tax obligations of citizen.

The wide-spread, legal bribery that asks states to cough up public money for placing or retaining company facilities in their jurisdictions must be recognized for what it is and eliminated by law at the national level. Bringing corporate tax revenues more in line with those of competitor nations needs to be central in crafting new corporate tax policies.

The idea of a corporate tax or credit system, based on carbon use or discharge, has much to recommend it, especially for the incentives it would provide for the technical reduction of global-warming gasses in the atmosphere. This issue is finally being recognized by many other nations as truly urgent. It should be given more urgent consideration in Congress.

A little-discussed problem associated with many of our biggest and most successful corporations is their escalating size and political power. Every week sees the merger of airlines, banks, movie producers, publishers etc. In these mergers and buyouts, efficiency and competitive power are increased but at a social price. The trend is hardly where the nation's internal economy and job structure needs to be going, even as international business competition must be considered. The current economic trajectory negatively impacts the urgent need for sufficient, middle class jobs in the United States.

The corporate merging process is most socially damaging in smaller American towns with a population big enough to support a big-box retailer that sells all kinds of products. When such a retailer comes to town, small businesses and their associated jobs disappear. The lower prices are great for residents but the result eliminates the variety of specialized retail stores and their employees that formed the social and economic bases of small town communities.

If the town cannot support another big box, the existing store is left without competition – the major thing that prevents price-gauging in the long term. Yes, a big box store in a small town is efficient and convenient but there is downward pressure on wages for any job in town and customers are not going to increase because the younger generations have to move to the cities to find jobs. Incoming companies with long term plans shun small towns for lack of amenities for their workers.

We are the unhappy observers of shrinking towns with fewer businesses and continuing concentration of workers in bigger and bigger cities. The evolution threatens the small town foundation of American culture and values. Better dispersion of industry out of growing mega-cities would be good for the nation.

Merging of commercial competitors into fewer and bigger corporations also means fewer but more powerful voices in the chambers of government. And with fewer, bigger, and more politically powerful commercial players across the country, who can rule out profitable agreements on cooperative pricing or retail hegemony in agreed-upon areas? Such corruption would be profitable but difficult and expensive for government to detect and prosecute.

In the case of huge investment banks, catastrophic failures have resulted in calls for limiting their size. 'Too big to fail' represents a danger to national and even world economies. We have seen such failures most recently in 1929 and 2008. The amounts of capital at risk in the speculative investments of the big investment banks are truly enormous and their functional interconnections constitute a potential danger for the nation's and world's financial systems if they fail. Although professionals in finance are good at what they do, their theoretical models and experience can never completely foresee the effects of mass psychology, stupid international actions, or the personal greed that can drive massive trading bets promising other-worldly profits.

A second reason to look askance at the size and complexity of incorporated investment banks, and other huge multifaceted corporations, is the difficulty of identifying legal responsibility for the many interrelated operations going on within them. The labyrinthine reporting and accountability in their business structures makes it difficult or impossible to indict individuals within the corporation for illegal actions documented by federal oversight authorities.

We have seen a noteworthy paucity of criminal judgments against individuals when oversight agencies present evidence of illegality, often of gigantic monetary proportions. If management cannot keep on top of everything because of institutional size and complexity, where does corporate accountability before the law reside?

As it did in the post-WWII decades, our government still retains an organizational framework that binds its citizens into cooperative endeavor and jealously protects the personal freedoms that our constitution guarantees. It is impossible for most of us to grasp the staggering scope of our government's varied functions and responsibilities. We have learned to expect spasms, gaffs, and countless shortcomings, even as we curse and vent over the many irritations encountered in dealing with the endless paper-work of government services and responsibilities.

It is unrealistic to complain bitterly about lack of efficiency, the type we expect of a company with a narrow, well-focused goal managed by a single person. Still, as hopelessly big and multifaceted as it is, the federal government is the *only* institution with the power and capability of creating a satisfying sense of national well-being.

In this book, I have argued that the current American economy is still economically capable of supporting a more fully employed and satisfied citizenry. Like so many before me, I point out that the federal government, to stimulate the economy and promote business investment and job creation, needs adequate financial resources with which to work toward the nation's betterment.

Because of the current political gridlock in Congress, the chance of accomplishing an overhaul of tax policy seems impossible. Our elected senators and representatives are too obsessed with the necessity of acquiring money for their next election. They also are too restricted in legislative action by money-empowered, central party control.

The political structure of our great nation is still in place, urgently needing just one major adjustment (getting special interest money out of the election process). Only when candidates for federal office can articulate a sense of how to achieve an inclusive government, sensitive to the needs of all, not just those of the super wealthy, should we listen to their positions on the many cultural, national, and international issues.

In comparison to the country that emerged from the Second World War as a world leader, America is now seriously faltering. We still have the means and national resources to be a great nation among nations. The central reason for this faltering is a federal government hamstrung by insufficient working revenues.

In this book I have shown that it is not the American economy or the wealth it provides that is the faltering problem. It is political. Republicans, in enforcing lowered tax policies to aid the economy, are starving our government of resources. Their policies have allowed much too much of U.S. working capital to be diverted into financial speculations for private wealth enhancement.

The data offered here indicates that such high corporate and personal profitability has little to do with GDP growth or job creation. Our Low tax policies are producing world class billionaires but a government whose solvency and services are falling behind those of other advanced nations. Each of us probably would define a 'great nation' in slightly different terms. I would be happy if we could again aspire to something related to the nation that emerged after the shock of WWII. Our economy then provided adequate jobs, a chance for an affordable education, and a decent life for most Americans. People with full time jobs earned enough to be independent of government subsidies. Poverty was relatively rare. Our government had sufficient revenues to provide high quality public amenities and strong support for the education, infrastructure, and science that enrich and enable our society and its economy.

Ours was a greatness of opportunity that left a legacy worthy of study and emulation. I believe we have the resources and talent to rise again.

GENERAL REFERENCES FOR FURTHER READING

Capital in the Twenty-First Century Thomas Piketty Belknap Press 2013

Keynes and Hayek: The Clash That Defined Modern Economics Nicholas Sapshott W.W. Norton and Company 2011

The Price of Inequality Joseph E. Stiglitz W.W. Norton and Company 2012

The Great Unravelling Paul Krugman W.W. Norton and Company 2003

Finance and the Good Society Robert J. Shiller Princeton University Press 2012

Our Kids Robert Putnam: The American Dream in Crisis Simon & Schuster 2015